Before Winter Comes

Before Winter Comes

A Journey on Horseback from Scotland to Cornwall

Cathleen Leonard

Before Winter Comes
A Journey on Horseback from Scotland to Cornwall

Copyright © 2019 Cathleen Leonard

Cover Image: Camping in Mudale, photo by the author
Cover Design created by the author using Kindle Cover Creator

The maps used in this book are licensed under Creative Commissions Attribution 3.0, and have been edited to show the route by Adriaan Kastelein. Maps originally created by Equestenebrarum.

Editing and proofreading by Sari Maydew and Linda Williamson

ISBN Paperback: 9781070129105

A Strange Request
www.AStrangeRequest.co.uk

www.facebook.com/AStrangeRequest

Printed by Amazon

In order to keep costs to a minimum, no photos have been included in the print version of this book.

To see photos from the journey, please visit:
www.AStrangeRequest.co.uk

Contents

Part 2: England

Acknowledgements

It's hard to know where to begin when it comes to thanking all the amazing people who have helped me in the pursuit of my dreams and in the writing of this book. It's harder still not to omit anyone in that process, but I will do my best.

Firstly, I would like to thank my long-suffering family for all their tolerance and support of my crazy dreams over the years. Next, I wish to thank my godmother, Wendy, for first giving me the opportunity to ride a horse and for encouraging me to pursue that passion. To Cate and Guy, for all your help and encouragement on my many adventures, thank you! Without you both I would never have made it as far as I have - I am forever indebted! To all my other friends, old and new, thank you for your support over the years as I struggled to muster the courage to set forth on this adventure. Your patience and understanding while I bored you silly with my incessant talk of equestrian travel is commendable. Thank you to the person – whose name I won't mention – who inadvertently pushed me so far that I finally bit the bullet and went after my dreams. If it hadn't been for you, I would never have set off. Thank you to CuChullaine O'Reilly of the Long Riders' Guild for all your support before, during, and after the journey. Thanks also to all the many Long Riders who have both directly and indirectly helped and inspired me over the years. To all the kind, welcoming, and hospitable people who offered us shelter and assistance on our way, thank you! Through your acts of kindness you have restored my faith in humanity and given me hope for the world: James and Carol Keith of Foinaven B&B in Durness; the man at Mudale who offered us a field; Doug Cambell of the Crask Inn; Alex near Lairg; Stacie MacDonald; the farmer at Croick Church; Sylvia and John at Ardross; Sian Llewellyn near Evanton; Claire and her family near Dingwall; Alex of Brahan Estate; Annie and Sweeney; the Wolf Man near Fort Augustus; the two men who stopped Spirit from starving on the shores of Loch Laggan; Mary and John near Loch Rannoch; Jason and Mel of Milton Eonan B&B; Rolf and Celia of Acharn Lodges, Killin; Tom, Jack and the other staff at Strathyre Holiday Lodges, Callander; the lovely staff at Applejacks Café in Callander; the kind lady in the chip van in Aberfoyle; Susie, Kirsty, and Laura of Gartmore; June of Strathblane; Fiona of Milndavie Farm Riding Centre; Davy and Fiona Gray; the staff at Windyedge Equestrian Centre; the two men in the horse lorry near Lanark; Maggie and Ian of the Clydesdale RDA group, and Sandra of the Scottish Equestrian Centre; the sheep farmer near Crawford and all the lovely people there who made me feel so welcome; Tom near Johnstonebridge; Vyv Wood Gee – mentor and inspiration; Ann, and the staff at Black Dyke Equestrian Centre; the lovely family near Scaleby Castle; Pamela Bonnick of Scalehouse Farm B&B; Alison Noble of Happy Hooves Riding Centre; the farmer at Bents Camping Barn; the farmer at Cowgill; the farmer near Wigglesworth; Cosima and Sir Simon Towneley; John of Birchenhead Farm in Wardle; Jen of Home Farm Livery; Janine Frost, and all the members of the Helen Atkin RDA group; Linda and Lissie; Johnny Meakin; Bob and Christina; Ed, Carolina and everyone at Valehead Farm; the staff at Country Treks; Jane Jones of Kyre RDA; Ellen Cochrane; Alan Sheppard; William Reddaway; Lisanne and all the staff at the Red Horse Foundation in Stroud; the staff at Wapley Riding Stables; Mickey and Tina Green; Anne of Wellow RDA; Anna Seymour of Redmond Bottom Livery Yard; Cheryl Green at Burrow Bridge; April Anderson; all the staff at the Conquest Centre; Lisa Walker, Pat, and Eric; Emma and Andrew Bowyer; Sarah Dawe. Thanks also to all the farriers who came out at such short notice to shoe Taliesin: Ian Mortimer of Tavistock; Keith Hedley of Invershin; Chris of Kirkintilloch; the farrier at Wardle whose name I have forgotten; and Jono Simpson at Bromyard. To my mother, Roxanne Leonard, and to my dear friend, Veryan Barneby, who patiently read this manuscript in its infancy and offered feedback, suggestions and lots of encouragement, thank you - and to Tony Hazzard for his feedback, too. To Adriaan Kastelein, thank you for all your work creating the maps of our route for the book. A huge thank you to Sari Maydew and Linda Williamson for their meticulous work editing and proofreading the manuscript to render it more readable. And thank you to Vlad for being so patient, supportive, and understanding throughout the creation of this book, and thank you for your unfaltering belief in me. Finally, I have to thank Taliesin and Spirit for accompanying me on this journey with such patience and tolerance. Their unwavering trust in me, and willingness to travel the length of the country without hesitation or complaint has utterly humbled me, earning them a very special place in my heart.

Part 1: Scotland

The route across Scotland

1

The Midges

'Taliesin*, stand still!' I said, exasperated, as I tried desperately to get the girth undone. The saddle and all my packs were dangling beneath his belly and he was beginning to fidget. His frustration was mounting and, any minute now, he was going to explode. I could feel it.

Anyone who has ever tried to undo a girth upside down on a horse will know how incredibly awkward a job that is - but if I didn't get this stuff off him in the next minute or so, not only would I lose my horse, but all the equipment I needed for the next few months would be destroyed as well.

Finally, I managed to undo the buckles. The saddle and all my gear fell to the ground with a heavy thud. I could hold Taliesin no longer. Letting go of the lead rope, I watched with dismay as he set off at a determined march back up the stony mountain track we'd come down the day before. He'd had enough.

I'd had enough too, and this was only the morning of the second day!

We were in the Scottish Highlands, one day and about twenty miles into our long journey home to Cornwall. It was the adventure of a lifetime, and a childhood dream finally being realised - except that

---

* For photos please visit www.AStrangeRequest.co.uk

losing my horse half way up a mountain in the back of beyond was not part of the dream. There is a vast difference between fantasy and reality. I should have known that by now.

The midges had arrived out of nowhere the night before as I was setting up camp. At first there were a handful hovering about, a mild nuisance. But within a matter of minutes more had arrived, and then more, and suddenly there were millions of the things. They were everywhere! My clothes became a seething mass of tiny, grey-black bodies, and every inch of bare skin was plastered. They got into my eyes, up my nose, inside my ears, down my neck, and up under my t-shirt. Everywhere they went they feasted, leaving my skin itchy, red and swollen. My face swelled up so badly I could barely see from beneath midge-bitten eyelids, and all I could hear was the hum of millions of minute wings as they swarmed about me, eager for a feed. The air around our camp had become a blue-grey, bloodthirsty cloud.

I took refuge in the tent with the few thousand midges that followed me in and set about executing mass murder, squashing them as best I could against the fabric of the walls and floor until nothing but a soggy mush of smeared midge remained. It was a losing battle and none of the insect repellent I had seemed to deter these creatures in the slightest.

I could hear poor old Taliesin outside the tent thundering up and down from one side of his crudely constructed paddock to the other, snorting with irritation and stopping only to rub furiously against the trees in a futile effort to relieve the unbearable itching. It was torture! To make matters worse he suffered with sweet-itch, a hyper-reaction to midge bites.

Even my wolfdog, Spirit, had fallen victim to the attack. The loathsome creatures had found where her coat was thinnest along her belly and around her nose. She lay in the tent looking miserable and fed up, her nose bleeding where she had been scratching it against her paws. I prayed the midges would disappear after nightfall and we could all get some much-needed rest. They aren't nocturnal creatures, surely?

Apparently Scottish midges are!

I didn't get much sleep that night, listening with a heavy heart to Taliesin running backwards and forwards, unable to escape his attackers, and wondering how long it would be before he broke through the electric fencing and disappeared off across the open mountainside. Yet by some miracle, he was still in his paddock in the morning when I eventually mustered up enough courage to stick my head out of the tent and into the buzzing cloud of eagerly awaiting midges.

I packed down camp, caught Taliesin, and, tying him to a tree, quickly began to tack up so we could get moving. The sooner the better! It was our only hope of getting rid of these infernal bloodsuckers, but Taliesin was fidgeting so much I couldn't even get his saddle on. Every time I put the blanket over his withers and went to lift my heavy Australian stock saddle up onto his back, he would swing his head round, lunging desperately at the heaving body of midges that plastered his flanks, and the blanket would slip off the other side.

At long last, and with great difficulty, I finally managed to get both the saddle and the blanket in place, loaded up all the gear, and we set off. I was leading Taliesin, who was pulling like a train, desperate to get away from the swarm of midges that followed in hot pursuit. He was a big, strong draught horse and I was struggling to hang onto him. We were half way down the track to the river when suddenly the saddle, packs and all, slipped round under Taliesin's belly. In my haste to get moving, I hadn't checked the girth! What a stupid mistake that was!

It is a testament to Taliesin's patience and sanity that, even under those stressful conditions, he didn't so much as flinch at all that stuff dangling underneath him - most horses I know would have panicked and bolted. But the minute I managed to free him of the load, he was off, and I couldn't hold him.

I watched as he strode determinedly up the mountain back the way we had come. He wanted to go home. I wanted to go home! What the hell was I doing out here? Why had I thought this would be a good idea?

2

The Dream

From the moment I first rode a horse, I dreamt that one day, that is how I would travel the world.

I was eight when, for a birthday present, my godmother had taken me riding on her little Welsh cob, Flurry. I fell instantly in love. To me, those powerful and majestic creatures, with their velvet-soft muzzles and gentle brown eyes, symbolised the ultimate freedom. They could carry me anywhere! From that day forward, my daydreams were filled with epic scenarios in which I rode a horse over wild mountains, through dark forests and across raging rivers, with a wolf at my side; setting forth on all kinds of magical quests and wielding a sword against nameless foes, like the heroes of myths and fairy tales. Sometimes in my daydreams I travelled in a horse-drawn wagon, foraging in the hedgerows, making lotions, potions and healing remedies from wild-gathered herbs. The scenarios were ever changing but the horse, the adventure, and the open road remained a constant and unwavering theme.

At some point in life, dreams, if dreamt for long enough, become plans; and plans, when executed well, become reality - except the bit about the sword. People aren't really allowed to charge around the countryside wielding swords, it's considered uncivilised and is generally frowned upon by the law.

Weapons aside, however, exploring the world on horseback was something I wanted to do. Every time I thought about it, it felt as though my heart had leapt into my throat and was expanding, choking me. I couldn't breathe. It was excitement and longing all mixed up into one overwhelming feeling - excitement at all the possibilities, the adventure and the unknown, and longing for beautiful landscapes and freedom! I spent hours poring over atlases, searching for the wildest, least populated places on the planet, linking up huge mountain ranges and working out how I might ride a horse around the whole of the world.

'It's impossible!' people said when I told them my dreams. 'It's the 21st century. No one travels on horseback anymore!'

I even half-believed them - although that wasn't going to stop me – until, at the age of fourteen, in some obscure corner of the World Wide Web, I stumbled upon the Long Riders' Guild website. What a glorious discovery that was!

Formed in 1994, the Long Riders' Guild was founded by a small group of people who had travelled thousands of miles on horseback, and who wanted to create a platform where advice, knowledge, and experience could be shared with the Long Riders of the future. Its many pages were brimming with tales of epic adventure, the world seen through the ears of a horse, explored slowly to the sound of steady hoof beats; thousands of miles across mountains, deserts and steppe, though jungles and deep, primeval forests, from the remotest places on the planet to the bustling streets of the metropolis.

As I read those stories with an insatiable curiosity, that ever-present feeling of excitement began to grow. Horseback travel was no longer a childish daydream, but a very real possibility being lived by a small, determined, and gloriously life-thirsty group of people across the globe.

One day, I resolved, I will become a member of that Guild!

That was all well and good except I didn't have a horse, and you can't travel the world on horseback without one. I contented myself with befriending other people's horses, pretending they were mine, and made the most of my weekly lessons at a local riding centre, imagining myself and the horse anywhere other than in a sand-school, going round and round in mind-numbing circles. As a result, I was never a very good rider, technically speaking. Getting a horse collected, working in an outline and making it perform intricate movements just didn't interest me. Neither did hopping over red and white painted poles. Riding through the open countryside, exploring the landscape, seeing what lay over that hill, in that valley, on the other side of that forest - that was where I wanted to be!

I was seventeen when I finally got my first pony.

I had spent a few years helping out with a neighbour's horse in return for riding, but when they eventually moved away I resolved to finally have a horse of my own.

I had worked hard at little part time jobs that fitted around my schoolwork - cleaning, dog-walking, house-sitting, washing dishes in a local pub - and had saved up enough money that I could afford to buy a horse and be able to keep it, too. In the end, realising that I had my heart set on the idea, my parents gave up trying to talk me out of it and so the search for my dream horse began.

My godmother, Wendy, was my go-to expert on horses. She'd had them all her life and she offered to help me in my quest. We scoured adverts on the Internet and drove miles to look at potential ponies. Some were too green, one was lame, another had a deformed hoof. And then we found Ailbhe (Elva).

Ailbhe was a pretty little Haflinger mare, standing no more than 14hh high, with a golden coat and a white mane and tail. She had a lot of scars, both physical and mental; her steering and brakes left much to be desired and she had a panic button that, when triggered, would send her running through even the thickest of hedges. She had been around the block a few times, passed from pillar to post, and was very mistrustful of people. As first ponies go, she was probably not the wisest choice for a novice owner!

We had gone to try Ailbhe one evening after school in the spring of 2008. I was nervous, and she felt tense and wound up when I rode her, as though at any moment she might panic and bolt. I knew immediately that her brakes and steering didn't amount to much - she had a hard mouth and didn't listen to my aids, but Wendy was tired of searching by this time and told me we could see a hundred more horses and still not find the perfect one, or we could just have this one. Fearful that my dreams of owning a horse might be snatched away from me, I agreed to buy Ailbhe, in spite of my unvoiced reservations, and a few days later she arrived.

We got off to a rather shaky start as I tried to work out how to ride this pony who didn't respond like the half-dead, push-button riding school horses I was used to. Over the years, Ailbhe taught me a great deal about horsemanship, often the hard way, yet with a commendable amount of patience, tolerance, and forgiveness. Gradually, she relaxed; we learnt to trust each other, and many blissful hours were spent roaming the countryside together around the family home in Hertfordshire, exploring lanes and bridleways, and galloping across the open fields. The freedom Ailbhe brought me was utterly intoxicating. This was true happiness!

Eight months after Ailbhe's arrival, whilst browsing the Internet for some cats to rescue, I ended up importing two little foals from France. They had been bred for meat and were being fattened for slaughter. At eighteen years old and an idealistic, headstrong vegan, with some slightly more black-and-white views of the world than I hold now, I went against everyone's advice and insisted that those two foals, who I couldn't get out of my head, were in no uncertain terms for me.

Of course I had no previous experience of handling youngsters, nor any idea about how to train them - but I was undeterred, and after the initial panic of finding two very real and rather feral foals being herded off a lorry and into my stable wore off, I set to work and somehow muddled through. I called those foals Taliesin (Tally-essin) and Oisín (Usheen). And suddenly here I was, with not one, but three horses, ready to take on the world.

3

Failed Attempts

School finished in 2010. Unsure of what to do with myself, I upped sticks and moved to Cornwall with my little herd of three horses in tow, and quickly settled into life working on a small-holding near Bodmin moor.

For the first few months the thrill of exploring unknown territory on horseback was almost enough to quell my burning desire for adventure. Wandering the maze of narrow, winding lanes, sunk deep between high stone-faced earth banks, was exciting; and galloping across barren, rock-strewn moorland was exhilarating. But once I knew what lay beyond that hill, in that valley, where that track led, my happy illusion of Bodmin moor being a boundless wilderness was eventually shattered. I came to realise that it was not a limitless expanse of rugged, mist-veiled tors, treacherous bogs, and bottomless pools steeped in legend, but was in fact a relatively small place, cut up by busy roads and scattered farms. Then that restless desire to head off on horseback came creeping back to tug at my imagination, and make my feet itch once more.

My first cautious steps along the rocky road towards horseback travel had been to spend a night out camping on the moor with Ailbhe. I tied a tent, a sleeping bag, and a few other odds and sods onto the saddle with baling twine (that most useful of things!), rode a mile or two up the road and passed an uncomfortable, sleepless night on the cold, hard ground, listening out for the sound of Ailbhe grazing, terrified that she would break loose and run off.

Ailbhe was totally unfazed and had taken the whole thing calmly in her stride, but I hadn't. I decided that night I didn't actually like camping, and I couldn't see myself doing it for any great length of time. I also realised that I really quite liked my nice comfortable bed, hot shower, and all the mod cons I had at home. So that was that. Dream over. Time to get on with real life!

However, real life was a rather boring and unappealing prospect. After recovering from my none-too-gentle run in with reality, the urge to swing up into the saddle and go trotting merrily off towards distant horizons returned.

So I tried again. I would ride around Cornwall, I decided. That would give me a good taste of life on the road. I spent weeks getting Ailbhe fit, took a month off work, and in June 2012 we set off. We didn't get very far. Actually we turned back after the first night - cold, wet, miserable, deflated, and once again resolved that this travelling on horseback lark was simply not for me. I wasn't cut out for it. I had given it my best shot and I was abandoning that dream once and for all!

And for a while, I did.

In 2013, at the age of twenty-two, I auditioned to become a fiddle player in a folk-rock band. For a few years my time was filled with festivals, gigs, tours, and weeks spent in studios writing and recording music. That life appeased my wanderlust by providing me with sufficient travel, plenty of thrills and adrenaline rushes, enough highs, lows, and creative stimulus to keep things interesting. The old call to adventure was quietened to the point that it became little more than a whisper, audible only in those rare moments of true, solitary silence. But it was still present, always there in the background, and the more I became aware of it the louder that call became.

A nasty bout of colic in the winter of 2014 took Ailbhe from me. The death of that sweet little mare shattered my heart in a way nothing else had ever done, but those two foals I had acquired on a crazy whim back in 2009...? Well, they had since grown up and were no longer little. In fact, they were now two solid and dependable draught horses, who were nearly as wide as they were tall and with enormous personalities to match. I had muddled through their training myself when they were about four years old and both had turned into surprisingly good mounts, which I think says a lot more about them than it does about my abilities as a trainer! With Ailbhe gone, it was time for Taliesin and Oisín to try their luck at making my dreams come true.

My collection of animals by this time had also grown to include a wolf - well, as close to one as you can get for a pet. Spirit was a Czechoslovakian Wolfdog crossed with a Northern Inuit – a dizzy combination of wolf, German Shepherd, Husky, and Malamute. She was beautiful, with a thick silver-grey and black coat that never seemed to stop shedding, and a playful, affectionate nature. She was an incredible escape artist who could open the most impossible enclosures or, failing to open them, could destroy them completely if she put her mind to it. She had an unhealthy taste for my tack, and within the first two years of having her, her count had reached two bridles, several pairs of reins, and two lots of girth straps. Other not so endearing qualities included a high prey drive, which made her a liability with most livestock and small animals; a strong aversion to other dogs; selective deafness if she was otherwise engaged in mischief - which no amount of training could cure - and to top it all off she had separation anxiety that made leaving her with anyone, for even a short period of time, an absolute nightmare.

As pets go, she was not the easiest, and as an adventure companion, she was far from ideal - but she certainly made life interesting and kept me on my toes, and I wouldn't have been without her.

In 2015, Taliesin, Spirit and I took to the moors with renewed determination for a life of adventure. Bodmin moor, then Dartmoor. One night, two nights, and still the conclusion was always that I didn't enjoy travelling like this; it was nowhere near as romantic as I had imagined. Riding off into the sunset usually boiled down to plodding about in the rain feeling cold, tired, and grumpy, trying to find somewhere to camp, and usually failing. Every time I asked someone for a field to camp in, I was either met with a flat no, or else offered a whole lot more than I had bargained for by over-amorous yokel farmers. Neither response filled me with a lot of confidence and I frequently ended up sneaking into a field for the night at dusk, and heading off again just after dawn, all the while terrified that I would be discovered by an irate landowner. How did my heroes from the Long Riders' Guild manage it?

In 2016, tired of failing to realise my dreams and sick of the unshakable, nagging call to adventure that continued to plague me, I finally mustered up enough courage and determination to ride to Land's End. It was only a hundred miles and I planned every overnight stop months ahead of time. Having people expecting my arrival not only meant that I didn't have the stress of finding a stop at the end of each day, but also that I risked losing face if I backed out without very good reason. It is amazing what you can achieve when you're worried about what other people might think of you!

I set out, rather appropriately, on the morning of the 1st of April, riding Oisín with Spirit trotting along beside us. Oisín had never actually been out camping before, but I naively assumed he would be just as relaxed as both Ailbhe and Taliesin had been on previous excursions.

I was wrong.

If you have ever tried travelling with a neurotic lunatic of a horse, then perhaps you'll understand. If you haven't, then think of all the destructive mania of a dog with separation anxiety. Now imagine a 1000kg horse with the same, and you have Oisín.

By the second night, Oisín had decided that I could not be let out of his sight for a single moment. If I so much as went round a corner, he would begin pacing up and down, neighing frantically at the top of his voice, sweating up, and trying to climb over the flimsy fencing of his enclosure until I came back into view. He wouldn't even let me go in my tent! In the end, I dragged my sleeping bag over to the fence and slept next to him, outside in the cold April rain.

That episode really helped to put sleeping in a tent into a whole new, and much more appealing light. We pushed on, Oisín settled down just enough that I could sleep in my tent, and after six long, tiring days, we finally reached Land's End.

Years of dreaming, several failed attempts, and a number of false starts later, I had finally done it! I had achieved what I set out to do: I had travelled on horseback, had tasted the dream, the open road and the world seen through the ears of a horse, and more importantly I had proved to myself that I could do it.

I travelled home from Land's End in the horsebox with Oisín and Spirit because Oisín had threatened a melt down at being left alone in the trailer. I hadn't minded that. It felt like a fitting end to the journey, to finish it as we had started - just me, my horse, and my wolf. I cried most of the way home, watching the landscape flashing past, landscape through which we had wandered slowly and steadily for the last six days. They were tears of happiness at having finally overcome the enormous mental block that had been holding me back from daring to live my dreams. A heavy weight had lifted; I felt free. When I unloaded Oisín from the trailer and led him quietly down the lane, where the high banks were adorned with the golden yellows of celandines, primroses and daffodils, blooming bright against a rich carpet of green, and bathed in warm spring sunlight that fell between the still bare branches of the trees, I was walking on air. Never have I experienced such an enormous sense of achievement, or so great an inner calm. That feeling was one of pure ecstasy.

A day or two later I began planning the next adventure. In July, less than three months after our return from Land's End, I set off again; this time with both Taliesin and Oisín. Three hundred miles around the South West of England, and of the twenty-three days we were on the road, there was only one where something didn't go wrong, and where I didn't think about throwing in the towel and going home. It was physically tough and mentally exhausting. Equipment broke, insects bit, girths rubbed, and one saddle had to be sent home after the first four days, leaving me to continue riding bareback and using my other saddle for all the gear. Routes that looked quiet and sensible on the map turned out to be main trunk roads for huge quarry machinery. Bridleways we needed to use were poorly marked or badly overgrown in some places, and on one occasion, Taliesin was even attacked by a swarm of bloodthirsty horse flies and ran off (who knew that would become a recurring theme?). Worst of all, we had two car crashes right under our noses.

The first happened when a van tried to overtake us at speed on a blind bend, just as another car rounded the corner. To avoid a head on collision, the car driver slammed on his brakes and another car hurtling up behind went straight into the back of him with a loud bang, a sickening crunch of metal, blaring horns, and a cloud of steam. To their credit, the horses merely flinched, did two strides of trot, and resumed their steady walk. The van driver, whose irresponsible driving had caused the accident in the first place, squeezed past the wreckage and disappeared off down the road. Fortunately no-one was hurt.

The next time we weren't so lucky.

Only a few days later, while making our way along a straight stretch of road under the North Wessex Downs, we saw a pair of cyclists approaching. There was a car waiting patiently behind them to overtake. Out of nowhere, another car came flying up behind it, braked too late, hit a bank and flipped over, not a hundred yards ahead of us. This time it was too much for the horses who spun around and set off back the way we had come at a flat out gallop. Without a saddle, I had no chance of staying on and fell down between the two horses, somehow managing to avoid their flying hooves.

Picking myself up, I jumped into the nearest car and told the startled-looking driver to follow my horses, who were leaving a trail of my trashed belongings strewn across the tarmac in their wake. We managed to overtake them about a mile down the road and I jumped out, caught hold of them, and calmed them down while some kind strangers gathered up all my things.

That finished me! I was giving up and going home, no more of this nonsense. I couldn't do it. I wasn't strong enough or tough enough to travel on horseback, and I just couldn't cope with everything the road threw at me.

That night, the people I was staying with sat me down after dinner and told me firmly that I had to keep going, if only for one more day. If I didn't, they said, I would never find the courage to do this again.

And so, more because I was afraid they would think me a terrible coward than anything else, I did carry on. For one day, two days, three - a whole week! Until Oisín suddenly became lame from a gash he had sustained to his heel bulb in the second accident. As luck would have it Lee, the owner of Woodhouse Farm Stables where we were staying, had just bought a horse lorry that morning and kindly offered to drive us home. It was an offer I couldn't refuse. I didn't have the will to push on, and besides, I couldn't with a lame horse!

The lame horse limped onto the lorry, and when we arrived back in Cornwall a few hours later and let down the ramp, he walked out as sound as they come! Not a limp in sight!

I had no sense of achievement and no elation when we arrived home this time, just a deep feeling of failure for having given up and not completed the ride I set out to do. The whole journey had been an uphill struggle, a harrowing test of my will and determination, and in the end it had all been too much. I was well and truly finished with this horseback travel thing! Never again was I going to let my imagination get the better of me and convince me to set off on another insane adventure - which definitely explains how, just over a year later, I found myself standing next to a pile of my equipment in the middle of nowhere in the north of Scotland, about as far from home as I could get on this island, watching my horse disappear off up a mountain!

4

Cashel Dhu

I waited for only a few despairing seconds and then set off up the track after Taliesin, thinking - hoping - he would stop when he reached the gate leading into the area of clear-felled forest through which we had come the day before.

He didn't.

Clearly still in a huff, he paused for a moment at the gate before veering off to the right, and continuing down along the fence line towards the shores of Loch Hope. The ground was wet and boggy, and there was a stream cutting across Taliesin's path. I thought perhaps he'd stop there; he is normally hesitant about crossing streams, but no! He hopped nimbly down the steep, muddy bank, waded merrily through the fast-flowing water, and clambered up the far side with an agility that I had never seen in him before. The ground became even boggier still and another stream barred his way, but that didn't slow him down a knot. He was on a mission! Why couldn't he walk at this speed and happily plough through streams when I actually wanted him to?

I upped my pace and splashed through the bogs and streams in his wake, getting muddy and soaked in the process. Eventually, I managed to catch up with Taliesin and get hold of his rope again. He almost looked relieved to be caught, because I don't think he had quite worked out where he was going or what he was going to do when he got there, but he had been hell-bent on proving a point.

He had proven it all right! I fully agreed with him about the direness of the situation, but what was there to do? It was no good going back to where I had left the saddle and packs lying in the middle of the track, because the midges were there, too. He wouldn't tolerate all that again. Poor Taliesin hadn't signed up for this adventure, so I owed it to him to respect his opinions and show some willingness to compromise in order to make his life a little easier.

I led him back through the streams and bogs, up to the gate into the fenced off area of forestry. Things were a little better up here. There was more of a breeze and distinctly fewer midges, but our gear was still a good half a mile back down the track and there was a lot of it. It would take me a while to carry it all up here, and given his current mood, I doubted Taliesin would stand around quietly while I did that.

So I did the only thing I could think of under the circumstances and, opening the gate, led Taliesin through it and let him go again. The forestry was enclosed, ringed by six-foot high, deer-proof fencing. I had no idea just how big the area was, or where Taliesin might end up, but at least I knew he would be in it somewhere.

Taliesin set off up the track, still in a huff, and I watched until he had vanished from sight.

Whose stupid idea had it been to start a long ride in Scotland? I was already regretting it and wishing I could go home. But I couldn't go home. I had made sure of that. Curse me for my foresight! I would have to see it through this time.

It was no good feeling sorry for myself and wallowing in self-pity. That wasn't going to get me anywhere. Taking a firm grip of myself, I banished all those crippling, negative, and utterly pointless thoughts from my mind, and set about lugging all the gear up to the gate; bit by bit, heavy armful after heavy armful, with Spirit following me patiently every step of the way.

It was a hard slog, all up hill, and it took me well over an hour. If I stopped to catch my breath, it wasn't long before the midges began emerging from the surrounding undergrowth for a feed; but at long last it was done, and my things lay piled up beside the gate. Now to retrieve my horse!

Spirit and I started off up the mountain, following Taliesin's hoof prints along the wide stony track. After a good mile or so we found him standing, gazing longingly over the gate that blocked his path on the far edge of the forestry. He had calmed down now and followed me placidly back to the pile of gear, where I managed to get him tacked up again. This time I made sure the girth was tight before we set off once more for the river and the ford at Cashel Dhu.

The ford was wide, and the water coloured such a rich red-brown from the peat in the surrounding hillsides that I couldn't see the bottom. It was impossible to tell how deep the river actually was. There were fresh tyre marks on the bank under Taliesin's hooves, however, that told me something had managed to get across the ford - and recently, too - so I pushed Taliesin forward, and to my surprise he went in with very little hesitation. The water came up to his belly as he splashed his way over the slippery rocks to the far bank, with Spirit swimming bravely alongside him. I was relieved to find the track again and even more relieved when we hit tarmac.

What a start to the adventure!

5

The Crask Inn

We followed the narrow road that climbed slowly up the valley along the foot of Ben Hope, whose black crags towered high above us. After a few miles, the road levelled out and began to drop steadily down again towards Altnaharra.

The scenery was bare. Open moorland rose gently to lone mountain peaks scattered across the vast horizons. Everything was big, spread out, and waterlogged. Ditches full of red-brown water became trickles that wound their way through peat bogs, gathering water and momentum, to become streams that tumbled down steep hillsides into red rivers. Here and there a loch glinted, iron grey under brooding but rainless skies. All was silent here in this watery expanse, save for the heavy, rhythmic fall of Taliesin's hooves.

Taliesin was tired so I led him most of the way, and whenever we stopped to admire the view or catch our breath his bottom lip drooped, his eyes glazed over, and he dozed off. I was tired too, so we stopped to rest often but briefly, driven on again by the ever-eager flocks of midges.

At the first sign of civilisation, a deer farm in Mudale, we halted and asked for a field for the night. I didn't fancy the idea of trying to wild camp if we were to be attacked again and I rather doubted that Taliesin would stick around to be eaten alive for a second night in a row. A large, well-fenced field was what we really needed!

The man who answered the door looked a bit confused when I told him what we were after, but soon rallied round, pointed me in the direction of an enormous field high on the windswept hillside, and sent me off with plenty of fresh water and a pocketful of fruit. There weren't nearly so many midges here, thanks to some regular gusts of wind. Nevertheless, as I set up camp, a small swarm materialised out of nowhere ready for a feast.

This time I was armed.

Earlier in the day, a couple of American cyclists on a tour of the Highlands had stopped to chat. I must have looked in a right old state with bites everywhere and my face still puffy and swollen, because before they left, they offered me some insect repellent which they swore actually worked and they also gave me a midge net - an ingenious invention, consisting of a fine green mesh that you pull down over your face and neck. The mesh is small enough to stop the midges biting while still allowing you to see, and although it does make you look rather comical, at this moment in time my appearance was an afterthought.

Thanks to that providential encounter with those kind cyclists, I managed to sit outside that evening and watch the sun go down over distant mountains, while I cooked a good, hot meal without actually becoming one myself!

The tent, however, was an entirely different story. When I had executed mass murder on several thousand midges the night before, the bodies of the fallen had stayed where they fell – smeared into the fabric of the tent and caked up in a thick black mush in all the corners. After a day spent rolled up on the back of a horse, the whole thing was now beginning to reek. The stench was overpowering! Worse yet, I was still blowing midges out of my nose and wiping them from the corners of my eyes. They were in my hair, my ears, and in every seam, fold, and pocket of my clothing. Now, I have no objection to going without a wash for a week or two, but even I drew the line at this. I desperately needed a shower and somewhere to wash my clothes!

As luck would have it, the Crask Inn, eleven miles away, had a room available for the following night. Even luckier still, they said they could accommodate my animals as well - and all for a pretty reasonable price. I didn't hesitate to book us in.

Oh the bliss of hot, running water washing away all remnants of the midges from my tired and itching body! I don't think I have ever been more grateful for a shower in my whole life. I savoured every moment of it as I washed the horrid black specks out of every conceivable nook and cranny of my anatomy, watching with disgusted fascination as they disappeared down the drain.

They had made good work of me! I surveyed the damage in the full-length mirror of my cosy little room in the inn. My face was still swollen, blotchy, and covered in bumps. I looked like a pockmarked adolescent and my chest, stomach and lower back were plastered in small, itching red lumps that strongly resembled chicken pox. I was not a pretty sight!

It was a splendid feeling being clean and dry and having a nice comfy bed to sleep in. My clothes were being washed and de-midged as well, by the kind landlord of the inn. This was luxury! I had only slept in the tent for three nights, yet here I was bolting for home comforts and mod cons at the first opportunity. I laughed. Clearly I was not as tough and wildly adventurous as I had imagined, and for a moment, just a moment, I felt a bit of a fraud; but the feeling soon passed.

Taliesin was happy in his nice paddock by the stream. It was quite exposed - most things in that bleak landscape were - and there was a good steady breeze blowing across the sweeping, open moorland, which meant that he could graze to his heart's content without being plagued by midges. There were some beautiful long-horned Highland cattle in the field next-door, with thick shaggy coats, and long ginger fringes that hid their docile brown eyes. Taliesin is very fond of cows and will quite happily stand gazing at them for hours on end with a soft, rather dazed expression, and that is precisely how I found him whenever I went out to check on him. He's a bit of an odd one, that horse, but he seemed content.

Back at the inn, on the small bookshelf in my bedroom that held no more than a dozen titles, I was delighted to find David R. Grant's

The Seven Year Hitch, which told the story of how, in the mid 90's, the author and his family had travelled around the world in a horse-drawn wagon. It was a book I had first come across through the Long Riders' Guild, and was one of many that had inspired me to live my dreams. In a roundabout sort of way, that very book had brought me to this moment in time - and by some strange stroke of Fate, here it was in a little inn in the middle of nowhere in the Scottish Highlands, in the very room in which I happened to be staying. Surely this had to be a good omen, a sign from the Universe that I was on the right track and that everything was going to be just fine - and if that wasn't a sign, then receiving an email that evening from the Long Riders' Guild offering their recognition and full support for my journey certainly was. My dream of becoming a member of the Guild lay within my grasp. All that stood between me and it were a mere 957.5 miles!

That email renewed my incentive and reinforced my determination to carry on. I didn't dare think about what lay ahead of us, or how far we had yet to go; nor did I know what tomorrow would bring or even where we'd be. All I knew was that we were here now, and that we simply had to take each day as it came.

I curled up in that nice comfy bed, in that cosy little room, in that inn in the middle of a wild and lonely landscape, and happily lost myself in a book all about somebody else's adventures.

6

The Feeling

Three months earlier, that old familiar feeling had hit me out of nowhere, catching me off guard and almost winding me. For a few seconds I could barely breathe.

It was the end of May, a cold rain was falling and I was out riding Oisín, with Spirit pacing along beside us, when I suddenly felt the urge, strong and overwhelming, to just keep on riding and never go home. Obviously I couldn't do that. I had responsibilities, a job, bills to pay - I couldn't just head off into the sunset on a whim. But it was tempting. Why it had hit me then and so strongly, as we plodded quietly around the narrow little Cornish lanes in the cold summer rain, I had no idea; but it didn't feel like it was going to go away any time soon.

After my experiences the year before, I had firmly resolved to stay home and forget about travelling on horseback - yet here I was, eager to hit the road again, ready to live the dream. And I knew where I wanted to go, too!

Somewhere down the line my daydreams about travelling through the wilderness on horseback, and my life-long love of mountains, had combined to form a goal: to ride across Scotland. I had never actually been to Scotland, but there were lots of mountains, an abundance of wild and rugged scenery, tumbling rivers, deep lochs and beautiful castles - if the pictures on shortbread tins were to be believed! It was the kind of landscape that evoked in me that familiar call to adventure and the irrepressible longing for freedom. It was probably more of a call to trouble, misery, and a whole lot of stress, if previous attempts at horseback adventures were anything to go on, but for whatever reason I just couldn't shake the feeling.

I had left home at nineteen full of dreams and plans for a wild and adventurous future. Instead, too scared to bite the bullet and chase those dreams, I had ended up drifting aimlessly along wherever the currents of life happened to take me.

Now here I was, twenty-six years old, still dossing about in the Cornish countryside, working menial part-time jobs that barely kept my head above water, feeling bored and utterly dissatisfied with life. There had to be more to it than this! Most people my age were on "career paths", settling down with partners, getting mortgages and popping out children left, right and centre. While none of those "real life" things actually appealed to me, I was beginning to get the uncomfortable feeling that life was whizzing past and I wasn't getting any closer to achieving the things I had set out to do. It felt as though my life were on standby, waiting for the great adventure that I didn't yet dare to begin. If I didn't do something soon, I was going to get stuck in this rut and before I knew it I would be old and bed-ridden, and those wild dreams of adventure would amount to nothing more than regrets.

I had been working in a pub in a small rural village. It was full of staunch regulars, most of whom had been born and raised within a twenty mile radius of the place, and who rarely left the county, never mind the country. Small places breed small minds, and small minds have narrow horizons. I saw the same old faces and heard the same conversations on repeat night after night - always the same people propping up the bar, sagely pronouncing judgement on a world that few of them had ever experienced. It was stifling and claustrophobic. What I saw there were people stuck in a rut, trapped in routines they didn't enjoy, working jobs they didn't like, to pay for things they didn't need, and at the end of the day - still dissatisfied with their lot - they turned to drink and idle gossip to fill the gaping void. They were not living, they were merely existing. Life was passing them by.

But life was passing me by too. I needed an escape! Throwing caution to the wind and heading off into the unknown in search of adventure is all well and good in daydreams, but the reality is a little bit more difficult, and whole lot more daunting. Surely it was better just to stay put within the confines of my comfort zone and stick at the daily slog?

There comes a point when familiarity, routine, security, and all the things that make up a comfort zone start to become anything other than comfortable, and you realise that the comfort zone is actually an anoxic, stagnant sort of a place which is slowly and surely suffocating you. I was at that point. Safety, comfort, routine, and familiarity had become the four walls of my cage and I was ready to break out, even though the idea was a truly terrifying one. But what terrified me even more, was the thought: what if I never do it?

Six weeks later I found myself sitting outside the horses' field gate. The sun was shining; it was a beautiful morning in mid July. I had my phone in my hand, finger hovering uncertainly over the dial button for Eric Gillie's Horse Transport. For the last time I asked myself, did I really want this? That all-too-familiar feeling of overwhelming excitement and longing welled up again, as it always did when my thoughts turned to horseback adventures, mixed now with a healthy dose of nerves.

I hit the button and booked the transport - a one-way ticket for one horse to Scotland. We would be leaving on the 22nd of August.

7

Castles and Graveyards

Spirit started to growl softly, the sound rising into a deep, warning bark as the footsteps approached across the gravel outside the tent.

We were camped next to a graveyard near Invershin and the light was beginning to fade. Who would be going to a cemetery at this time of night? It wasn't like Spirit to bark. My heart began to thump.

Cautiously, I stuck my head out of the tent into the obligatory cloud of midges and found myself looking at a dark-haired man wearing blue overalls and carrying a rake. He had eyes that looked in different directions, but he seemed alright.

Spirit continued to bark her warning and I didn't stop her, but I greeted the man cheerfully and asked whether he thought anyone would mind us camping there.

'Well I doubt you'll disturb the neighbours!' he joked, in a soft Highland accent.

'What about the horse?' I had slipped Taliesin into the field next door. It was empty and had recently been cut for silage. I hadn't thought anyone would mind.

'Aye, I'm sure it's nae bother. I doubt anyone will even notice.' The man seemed pretty friendly and relaxed. Spirit stopped barking.

We had set off from the Crask Inn that morning, feeling clean, well-rested and blissfully midge-free! The road from the Inn led across more desolate and uninhabited moorland. Here and there large swathes of dark evergreen forestry were scattered across the bleak landscape, becoming more frequent and condensed as we approached Lairg. There wasn't much in Lairg so we didn't stop, and after crossing the bridge over the tail end of Loch Shin, we picked up a quiet road that followed the River Shin along a steep valley between thickly forested hillsides.

After a few miles, the valley opened up ahead of us, wide and shallow between small hills. There were a few fields about and, having covered the best part of twenty miles that day, I felt it was time to stop for the night.

We didn't see a soul at the handful of scattered houses that made up the hamlet of Inveran, nor was there anyone at the little village hall that we passed. The road looked like it was heading into yet another large area of forestry, so when I saw the cemetery and the large, empty field next to it, I decided we had better try our luck and see if we could get permission to camp.

I began knocking on doors, and eventually found a deaf man who quite understandably failed to comprehend my very best, but utterly futile attempts to communicate my question through the medium of mime. Try explaining to someone without using words that you're looking for a field to camp in for the night with a horse, and you'll probably see the difficulty.

In the end I gave up and decided to chance it. It was too late to push on anyway.

'What's that?' I now asked my new friend, pointing to a rather foreboding old castle that loomed grey above the trees in the fading light further down the valley.

'That's Carbisdale Castle,' he said. 'Known locally as the Castle of Spite.'

An intriguing name!

It had been built for the Duchess of Sutherland in the early 1900's, he told me, after a family dispute over the will of the late Duke had ended with the Sutherland family agreeing to build the Duchess a castle on the condition that it was outside the Sutherland lands. The Duchess had the castle built on a hill right on the edge of their lands, overlooking the railway and the road, where the family would be forced to pass in its shadow every time they journeyed to and from Sutherland. She'd had clocks placed on three sides of the castle tower, but the fourth side, which faced Sutherland, she left bare because she wouldn't give the family the time of day; and thus the castle became known as the Castle of Spite. It was certainly a good story.

That night I dreamt that a little old lady from the cemetery was peering at me over her knitting and telling me very sternly that I shouldn't be there. In spite of that, I slept soundly.

The following night we once again found ourselves camping next to a graveyard at the end of a long road that had brought us up the beautiful Strathcarron. The clustered houses at the mouth of the valley near Bonar Bridge had given way to increasingly scattered farms and acres of green fields. As we climbed steadily along the course of the river, the farms petered out and we passed picturesque lodges tucked in among thick woodland, which in turn gave way to open hilltops that were a colourful patchwork of purple heather, yellow-green bracken and wind-browned grasses, brightly illuminated in places by ever-moving gaps in the scudding grey clouds.

In Glencalvie, at the head of the valley where the road ended, we found Croick church, and a kindly farmer who offered us the use of his field next to the graveyard.

At a glance Croick church is an unassuming little white-washed stone building, sheltered by a stand of weather hardened trees among which lie a smattering of old headstones. On closer inspection, however, that little church way up there at the head of a long valley, set against a dramatic backdrop of mountains, holds a bitter tale of human suffering.

Towards the end of the 1700's land owners in the Highlands decided that, with a growing demand for wool, grazing sheep was a more profitable business than tenanted subsistence farming and the local crofters were forcibly evicted from the lands they had been working for centuries.

The Highland Clearances, which happened over the course of a hundred years throughout the north of Scotland, saw tens of thousands of families ousted, often violently, from homes that had been theirs for generations. Crofts were burned to the ground to prevent their previous inhabitants from returning, forcing families to move away. Some relocated to southern or coastal regions, while many emigrated to the Americas and Australasia, either voluntarily, or forced to do so by their former landlords; and some, too old and frail to endure such upheavals, died of cold or starvation. It was a bitter time for the people of Scotland.

During the clearances that took place in Glencalvie in the spring of 1845, with nowhere else to go, some ninety-odd people took up residence in the churchyard at Croick in a crudely constructed shelter of tarpaulins and poles. Messages left by those people can, to this day, still be seen scratched into the east window of the church. They serve as a poignant reminder of that dark period in Scotland's history that saw thousands of people dispossessed of their lands in order to make way for sheep that would serve to better line the pockets of indifferent landowners. No record exists of what happened to the people who took refuge there at Croick.

Other messages etched into the windowpanes of the church refer to further events which took place in Strathcarron. Some nine years after the clearance of Glencalvie, just a few miles back down the valley at Greenyards, the last remaining tenant families were finally, and brutally, evicted in what was dubbed the Massacre of the Rosses.

Faced with imminent extrusion, and having already resisted several attempts to serve them with eviction notices, a group comprising mostly of women had met the band of forty-strong constables sent to remove them from their homes. The women had been violently set upon by the officers, beaten and kicked into submission, and left lying at the roadside while the constables proceeded to burn down their houses.

Looking around at this beautiful, tranquil place it was hard to imagine that the seemingly untouched, empty landscape had once supported so many families, and it was harder still to imagine the despair those people must have felt during those dark times.

I awoke to the clatter of falling rocks. Scrambling out of the tent, I saw Taliesin standing nonchalantly amongst the scattered remains of a section of dry-stone wall, happily munching the grass on the other side.

There was plenty of good, lush grass on his side of the wall, and he was making no effort to escape across the rubble so I suspected that Taliesin was simply taking a bit of a stand and protesting the fact that he had been plucked unceremoniously from his comfortable life in a field back in Cornwall, piled onto a lorry bound for Scotland, and was now being made to walk the thousand-odd miles back to where he'd started. And all this without his permission! No wonder he was feeling peeved.

When deciding which horse to take on the journey, Taliesin had been the obvious choice given Oisín's antics on our little excursion to Land's End back in 2016. I hadn't wanted to travel with two horses again - it was too much hassle, and too expensive, so Taliesin it had to be. As horses go, he's a pretty phlegmatic sort with a philosophical approach to life and a calm, sensible nature, who generally accepts the world as he finds it, taking everything in his great, lumbering stride. It takes a lot to get Taliesin really het up, but once riled he's incredibly strong and determined, and there's absolutely no reasoning with him until he's calmed down. God help me if he really got it into his head that this adventure was not his cup of tea!

It had been something of a gamble, but at least I would be able to sleep in a tent and go out of sight for more than a few minutes without him losing his head over it. So far, it seemed, I had made a good choice. Barring that first ghastly episode with the midges, Taliesin was proving to be a very tolerant travel companion and had complained very little indeed.

I thought back to that rainy January night in 2009 when the transporter had arrived from France, herded two tired and scared little foals into my stable, and then vanished into the night leaving me wondering what on earth I had done.

Oisín had been easy to handle. Ruled by his stomach and with enough lice to encourage him to seek out the benefits of human contact, I had managed to get a head collar on him the very next morning. Within a few days he was leading around quietly as though he'd been doing it his whole life. Taliesin, on the other hand, had been utterly terrified of humans and spent the first week or so hiding behind Oisín whenever anyone came near. Food had not been a motivating factor, nor had scratches, even though he was a sack of bones and riddled with lice; but with time and patience, we got there in the end.

I had first stumbled across their photographs on the website of a charity advertising horses in France that were destined for slaughter. There were old horses who were past their prime, injured horses who were no longer deemed "useful", race horses who hadn't made the time, and foals ... lots of little foals brimming with unexplored potential.

I flicked through all the photos of hopeless, heart-broken looking horses with a lump in my throat, thinking of those beautiful animals abandoned by the people to whom they had given their absolute best, the people they had trusted, and who had repaid their years of dedicated service by sending them to the meat farm to await certain death. And that death would be neither quick, nor without trauma, as many of these horses ended their lives in Italian slaughterhouses after days spent on a lorry being transported in cramped conditions with neither food, nor water, nor rest. Many didn't survive the journey. The thought was unbearable. I had to do something. Surely I could help one of these horses?

'You can't have another horse!' my parents told me flatly. 'You've already got one. You'll be putting a millstone around your neck if you take on any more.'

'You don't know what you're getting. They were bred for meat. They could have all sorts of health problems, conformation issues or bad temperaments,' my godmother warned me. 'If you want to rescue a horse there are plenty here in England that need rehoming.'

But I didn't want another horse - I wanted one of those horses!

Of all the horses, there were two that stood out from the rest: a spirited-looking bright bay foal with a white five-pointed star on his brow and little black socks, and the forlorn-looking chestnut with a dark blond mane and tail and a large white diamond in the middle of his forehead. There was something about those foals, something special. I could feel it, and I just couldn't get them out of my head. So, ignoring the sound and sensible advice of my godmother, and my parents' objections to the idea, I cleared out my bank account and got the two foals anyway because it felt right. I can honestly say that to this day, it is the best thing I have ever done and I have never regretted it for a moment.

All that seemed like only yesterday. Where had the time gone? And how had that little sack of bones with the five-pointed star, who had hidden, shaking, behind his companion all those years ago, grown into this enormous lumbering bear of a horse that was now going about tearing down stone walls with his tree-trunk sized legs and dinner-plate hooves in the wilds of Scotland? We had come a long way, he and I, and I adored him - even if he had just trashed a wall that was going to take me the best part of an hour to rebuild.

I sighed, lovingly called Taliesin a whole load of horrible names, threatened to sell him for Tesco's lasagne, then set to refitting the stones painstakingly back into the wall, one by one. Taliesin looked on with an air of solemn interest, unmoved by my threats of the supermarket freezer aisle, and a small cloud of midges descended to feast on whatever piece of me they could get to.

We abandoned tarmac roads that day and headed up into the mountains, following tracks across the Glencalvie estate through sheep and deer filled pastures.

A solitary Highland pony named Kayleigh, who was grazing in one of the fields, took an instant liking to Taliesin and he to her. She desperately wanted to come with us and looked crestfallen when I closed the gate behind us and led Taliesin away up the mountain. He cast her several long, backward glances and the odd whinny, and then forgot all about her as soon as she was out of sight. It was a short-lived romance.

We made our slow and steady way along the course of a little stream on whose banks grew a smattering of old birch trees, draped in wispy silver-grey moss. There were cattle grids along the track, and lots of them! Some had no side gate, or if they had it was too small for

Taliesin's large frame to squeeze through with all the gear piled on him. Luckily the rungs of the cattle grids were close enough together, and his hooves large enough, that he could walk right across them - and he did, without batting an eye.

It started to rain lightly and a cloud of little black flies that I had never seen before, but which had a nasty bite, descended on us and made life hell for a while, and the silence of that beautiful glen was broken by my curses and wildly flailing arms as I did battle with the swarm until we broke through the tree line and the wind picked up again.

We passed some men putting up a deer fence half way up the mountain. One was driving long posts into the ground, while the other two grappled with great rolls of wire sheep netting. All were midge-proofed up to the eyeballs and not a word was said about the fact that it was a dull and drizzly morning, but they did comment that it was very 'midgey' out.

Midges are to the Scottish what the weather is to the English: a safe and easy conversation starter and a good topic to fall back on in socially awkward situations. Virtually no conversation I had with anyone in Scotland went without the subject being touched upon. There were even midge forecasts given for the Highlands and the people in the west maintained that is was less 'midgey' there than it was in the east, and the people in the east thought themselves fortunate because the midges were far worse in the west, and I can honestly say that I didn't notice any difference at all.

The weather, which - unlike the midges - seemed rarely to come up in conversation, was changing almost from one minute to the next as we made our way up the glen. Thick clouds tumbled silently down the surrounding hillsides, bringing with them a steady, cold drizzle, only to lift again revealing row upon row of jagged mountain peaks stretching away to the horizon on all sides, and then they would vanish as the clouds rolled in to envelop us once more.

The track skirted the top of a mountain overlooking beautiful Glencalvie and then began a long descent into Strath Rusdale, through acres of boggy forestry that was being steadily felled all up the valley. The hillsides here were stripped bare to a wasteland of rotting tree stumps and branches, which stood out like an open wound on the landscape. But even in that wasteland new life was beginning, and coarse heather, purple foxgloves and little saplings of native trees were springing up amongst the fallen debris.

Finally, at the end of what had been a long and tiring day, a lovely couple at Ardross took us in and gave Taliesin the field in front of their house for the night, where he immediately set about trying to bring down the telegraph pole with his vigorous scratching. He followed that up with eating some old grass cuttings that he sniffed out from among the rich new growth of grass and reeds. It was a bad move on his part. Grass cuttings can kill a horse, and I wondered if it was a conscious act of self-destruction, intended to prove yet another point about how he was feeling about his lot.

I decided, rather hard-heartedly, that he would either live or die and I would have to wait till the morning to see which it was, because dashed if I was going to call a vet to pump his stomach if he was stupid enough to eat grass cuttings when there was enough good grazing about!

Leaving him to it, I went to soak away my aches and pains in a wonderfully hot bath, and my kind hosts washed my dirty, sweat-soaked travel clothes. While my clothes dried, those beautiful people fed me a plate piled high with rice and steaming vegetables freshly picked from their little garden behind the house.

To my relief, Taliesin was still alive when I finally tumbled into my tent and fell asleep; clean, well fed, and basking in the warmth and hospitality of those two complete strangers, my faith in humanity full to the brim.

8

Rejection

My recently restored faith in humanity had taken a sudden
knock. It was inevitable, I suppose, that at some point I
would meet some less than welcoming and not-so-lovely
people on my journey. Nevertheless, the rejection and absolute
disinterest left me feeling like the carpet had been whipped out from
under me. This was a new sensation and I didn't care for it much.

It had been a long day that had seen us get hopelessly lost when I'd
opted to leave the busy main road into Evanton with its speeding,
impatient drivers, huge lorries and strings of noisy motorbikes, in
favour of quiet forest tracks through the Novar Estate. After going
round and round in frustrating circles trying to navigate the dizzying
maze of criss-crossing tracks, we had eventually emerged in Evanton
little more than two miles from where we had left the main road
several hours before. From there, we followed a back road to
Dingwall, where we did a rather unnerving stretch on the ring road
around the town in the middle of rush hour which involved a hair-
raising few minutes waiting at some traffic lights in the middle lane
while cars sped by us on both sides. To his credit, Taliesin didn't so
much as twitch an ear at any of it because he's an amazing horse really,
with nerves of steel, who saves his protestations for more appropriate
moments.

I was relieved when we finally escaped the mayhem of town, abandoning the traffic-heavy trunk roads in favour of a quiet lane that led through another large estate.

The land around Dingwall seemed to be mostly arable. There were acres and acres of golden wheat fields, through which huge combine harvesters crawled, spitting out ripe wheat kernels into high-sided trailers hauled by enormous tractors, and leaving neat rows of straw in their wake, ready for baling. There wasn't a green field or a paddock in sight!

It was getting late, we had covered over twenty miles already and were all tired, hungry, and ready to finish for the day. I was growing anxious and beginning to wonder whether we'd find anywhere to stop for the night when suddenly, there in the midst of a golden sea of cornfields, we came upon a riding centre! My heart leapt. Thank goodness! Horsey people! Surely they would be able to help us out.

A tall balding man with a beard, who was standing in the yard smoking a pipe, pointed me in the direction of the indoor arena where the yard owner was giving a lesson.

'Make sure you apologise before you say anything else!' he called out with a grin and a wink as I headed up towards the arena, leaving my animals with one of the yard girls. 'She's a bit of a dragon!'

I knocked on the door of the gallery and let myself in. A woman was sitting on a chair barking instructions at a young man going round and round in tight circles on a nice-looking red roan pony. She was slim, sour-faced, with short brown hair cut into a bob, and she looked to be somewhere in her forties. She did not seem amused at being interrupted mid-lesson and I withered a little inside as she looked me up and down with an air of utter disdain.

This was not a good start.

'No,' she snapped when I tentatively, and apologetically, enquired whether she knew of anywhere nearby that we might camp for the night. 'There are no fields around here. I've no room either. It's too late to sort anything out now. I don't have time to move all the horses around. You had best keep going!'

'Do you know of anywhere nearby we can try?' I asked, without much hope

'No.' At least she was to the point.

The next village was still a good five miles away on the far side of the estate. It was a long way to go, and what if we didn't find anywhere to camp there either?

'What about the estate? Do you think they might have a field we could camp in for the night?' I tried again.

'No,' she said decisively, turning back to her student.

'Well, can we at least get through the estate?' I asked, beginning to feel more than a little disheartened. 'Are there any locked gates I need to know about? Do I need to back-track and follow the main road?'

'We ride on the estate but I don't think they'll like you riding across it!' she said, rather haughtily. The man was right she was something of a dragon.

I was getting nowhere. All the happiness and faith in humanity that had filled me the night before was quickly fading away. This woman was being so incredibly unhelpful to the point of being nasty, and at the end of a long day my guard was down and it was starting to get to me.

My face must have belied my rapidly vanishing optimism because, as I turned to leave the gallery, she softened a little and said she could ring the estate office to ask if maybe they had a field free - stressing, however, that she highly doubted it.

I felt a glimmer of hope returning. Perhaps she wasn't so bad after all.

The phone rang and I heard the girl on the other end say that everyone had left for the day, that she wasn't in a position to say whether I could camp or not, but that she could pass on the number for the estate manager if we liked. I felt more hopeful still, but to my horror this sour-faced old dragon told her not to bother, hung up and turned to me with a shrug as if to say she'd done her bit and there was nothing else she could do.

There's nothing worse than getting your hopes up only to have them dashed by people who decide that you're not their problem and that they don't care. It's the rejection, the feeling that you are insignificant and of no importance that hurts. Of course this woman was under no obligation to help me, I knew that, and I certainly didn't expect help from anyone, but surely there was no need to be quite so unkind about it, so cold and hard-hearted? Her apathy and dismissiveness had taken me completely by surprise and knocked me sideways off my otherwise steady course.

I retrieved my weary animals and set off again, waiting until I had rounded the bend in the road before I broke down in tears. I was tired, fed up, and I didn't know what to do or where to go, and sometimes it's just nice to let it all out.

Feeling a whole lot better, I picked myself up and dusted myself off, reminding myself that there were lots of kind and helpful people out there in the big wide world, and that we'd met plenty of them on the journey so far. So we pushed on further into the estate.

No more than a mile down the road, at the first row of cottages we came to, we met a friendly woman named Clare. She fetched Spirit a bowl of water and then found me the number for the estate keeper, who in turn put me onto the estate owner, and he told me I was more than welcome to camp anywhere on the estate that took my fancy. So I put Taliesin into the very next field we came to, which was full of long grass, and he happily set to eating while I put up the tent. Then I spent a pleasant evening with Clare and her three children, chatting and drinking tea, while Spirit made herself quite at home on the sofa. She was thoroughly enjoying being petted and fussed over - so much so that she looked utterly crestfallen when it came time to leave. And that lovely family, through their easy-going kindness, once again restored my faith in humanity and made me feel that all was right with the world.

9

Leaving

We had been on the road for a whole week now, but already it felt like a lifetime since I had forsaken my easy existence back in Cornwall to head off in pursuit of my wildest dreams. Letting go of all that was familiar and comfortable, breaking away from my safety net of friends and heading off to a place hundreds of miles away where I knew nothing and nobody, was one of the hardest things I have ever done.

Many people have dreams, a longing for adventure and an innate soul-calling to wander the wild places of the world, but most lack the courage - or perhaps the stupidity - to bring those dreams to life. And I could understand why! Dreaming is all very well, but the reality is a truly intimidating prospect.

'Do you think when you've done this, that will be it and you'll finally settle down?' my mother had asked me hopefully, a few weeks before I was due to set off. She was anxious about the journey and hadn't been too keen on my previous solo excursions. A young woman travelling alone and sleeping rough in a tent, miles from anywhere? People would tell you that this was asking for trouble, although they never say the same about young men! Well people can go stick it, because I refuse to let my age or gender dictate what I may and may not do with my life.

Even so, I was nervous. It would be stupid not to be. There was an awful lot that could go wrong, both for me and for my animals. If I fell off and injured myself, how would I get help? If Taliesin ran off in the night, how would I find him? If my animals got hurt, what would I do then? What if there was a car accident again? It was dangerous; there was no arguing that. But I also reasoned that everyday life is a series of calculated risks, and that most of the things I was worried about could just as easily happen within the supposed 'safety' of my comfort zone. It was merely the familiarity of my surroundings that made those risks appear somehow less. No, I couldn't chicken out on those grounds!

As our departure grew imminent, people began asking me whether I was looking forward to the journey. Was I excited? Nervous? I tried to field those questions, put on a nonchalant front and feign a positivity that I didn't really feel. Inside I was petrified, fighting to hold back the rising surge of panic that threatened to envelop and drown me at any moment. My answer to this barely manageable anxiety and dread had been to flatly refuse to think about what lay ahead, to focus solely on the here and now, and to deal only with the immediate daily tasks - marking down my route on the steadily growing pile of maps that arrived in the post each day, checking over equipment, organising and packing the gear, and getting Taliesin, Spirit, and myself fit for the ride. Beyond that, I dared not think.

In those final days before leaving, I withdrew into myself - so terrified that I couldn't think about anything much at all. All the safety, comfort, routine and familiarity that I had been so eager to abandon in favour of wild adventure, now held a new and very strong appeal; offering a security to which I desperately wanted to cling. But it was too late. I was committed. I was going.

The 22nd of August arrived and so did the transporter. I put on a brave face, loaded Taliesin into the lorry and watched with a lump in my throat as it pulled away down the road. I wouldn't see him again until we met in the north of Scotland three days hence. My heart nearly broke when I heard Taliesin neigh, confused and scared at finding himself alone in a lorry being taken to God-knows-where. I wondered what was going through his head, if he thought maybe I had sold him, abandoned him, sent him away. I could have cried then. I wanted to, but I didn't dare. If I broke now that would be it, I would never leave, never go after my dreams and I'd spend my life wondering 'What if...?' And besides, Taliesin was gone now, winging his way up to Scotland. I had no choice but to follow.

I wasn't allowed to ride up in the lorry with Taliesin - something about insurance. Instead, a few staunchly supportive friends had rallied round and kindly offered to drive me, Spirit, and all our gear up to the north of Scotland, over the course of the next few days.

The first was Cate, who took us as far as Glastonbury. A close friend and confidante, Cate had been an unwavering source of encouragement to me in my mad dreams and had always offered help and support in any way that she possibly could. She's a strong, independent sort of person, with a pretty low tolerance for nonsense. She has a zest for life and her motto is: "It's not the dress rehearsal!" I love Cate for her honesty and authenticity. Starting the journey with her gave my fragile confidence a much-needed boost.

In Glastonbury we met up with Guy, who had offered to drive us the rest of the way. I had met Guy several years earlier when playing at a festival in the Netherlands with the band. He had made firm friends with us all and had often come to see us at gigs back in the U.K. Guy is a real gentleman and the sort of person who would do anything to help anyone. I have always said that if you were stuck in the middle of nowhere in the middle of the night and needed rescuing, Guy would be the man to call. He had helped me a lot on my ride around the South West the year before, so it felt somehow fitting that he should once again be assisting me on my adventures.

It took us two days to reach our destination, and as we drove across the landscape through which I would soon be travelling I felt a stirring of excitement, intermingled with that ever present feeling of sheer panic, at the thought of riding over those hills and through those forests, exploring what they had to offer. This was my dream, after all. Was it really, finally going to happen? And then I wondered doubtfully whether I would make it. It didn't seem possible. I was a dreamer, a fantasist. I would never be able to cope with the reality of life on the road. What on earth was I doing? The panic surged, threatening to overwhelm me, so I shut it out and tried to think of anything else.

Guy was a wonderful distraction from my trepidation, chatting happily about the many exciting things he'd been doing with his life, but as we neared our destination, a tense silence descended in the car. There was a knot in my stomach that had been gradually getting tighter over the course of the last few days. I felt sick and I couldn't make light-hearted conversation anymore. The inevitable moment of departure was approaching; the harsh reality was about to begin.

I had decided to start in Scotland for two reasons. Firstly, it was quite late in the summer by the time I had mustered enough courage to commit to the journey, and I knew that the weather would be getting progressively worse as autumn wore on; and the other, more important reason was that if I set off from the furthest point on the journey, then each day would bring me a few miles closer to home. I was more likely to succeed this way, and I wouldn't be able to just give up and go home on a whim at the first sign of trouble, because home was too far away and transport was too expensive. Sometimes you have to outsmart yourself and fool-proof your plans against the devious, cowardly side of your own nature. I understood myself well enough to know that I had to plunge in at the deep end in order to make myself swim.

The most logical place to start the journey would, of course, have been John O'Groats, the northernmost point on mainland Britain, with Land's End as the finish line. That's what most people do. But everyone I spoke to said John O'Groats is a pretty bleak place and to give it a miss. The northwest, they said, was much more picturesque. Since I had no intention of riding to Land's End again once I reached Cornwall, and this wasn't going to be yet another end-to-end journey, I settled on Durness, the most north-westerly town on the mainland, as our starting point. I'd emailed a few local B&Bs until someone agreed to let me unload Taliesin and graze him overnight in their field, and that was that.

We arrived in Durness late in the afternoon of the 24th of August, unloaded all the gear from Guy's car, got my tent set up behind Foinavan B&B - where James and Carol Keith had kindly offered me the use of their field for a night - and then went to have dinner at the local pub while we waited for Taliesin to arrive. I fear I was not good company for poor old Guy, who had given up four days of his time to do the round trip from Glastonbury to Durness, and all the way back again; but I trusted he knew me well enough to understand that my silence was not born of rudeness or a lack of gratitude, but rather from the terror and insecurity that I was trying desperately not to let show.

The lorry arrived late and Taliesin staggered off the back, looking dazed and exhausted after his long journey up. I turned him out into the pasture and looked on with apprehension as he made straight for the telegraph pole, pitched his whole weight against it and began rubbing his tail furiously until the pole shook and I feared he would bring it down, wires and all.

With Taliesin settled for the night it was time for Guy to leave. I didn't want him to go. He was my last piece of familiarity and my only friend here at the end of the world where I didn't know a soul. But there was no reason for him to hang around, so I gave him a big hug that probably told him more about my emotional state than I had dared to let on, thanked him from the bottom of my heart for bringing me and Spirit all the way up here, and tried to sound optimistic about what lay ahead. I waved him off down the narrow road that wound away through the barren mountains, before heading back to my tent. Suddenly I felt very much alone.

An early start after a restless night saw us set off along the main road, through the scattered collection of houses which made up the village of Durness. It was the height of tourist season and the winding, single-track road would soon be awash with cars, caravans, motorbikes and cyclists. Taliesin wasn't a great lover of motorbikes, or those cyclists who sneak up silently from behind and suddenly flash past with no warning, scaring the living daylights out of both horse and rider, so I was keen to get as many miles behind us as we could before the roads became busy.

I was feeling surprisingly calm as Taliesin strode through the near-deserted village and out past the last few straggling houses along the coast road. He was still looking a little dazed but somehow the familiarity of being ridden seemed to calm him and bring him comfort, and the feeling of being back in the saddle reassured me too. This, at least, we knew how to do.

The day had dawned gloomy and overcast, but the clouds were high and the views incredible. The sea stretched calm and grey to the north, while rugged mountain peaks loomed against grey skies to the south. Boggy, rock-strewn hills clad in purple heather rose up to our right, and to our left the land fell sharply away to the shores of Loch Eriboll on which the clouds, dark with the threat of rain, were reflected against fathomless depths. Every now and then, a beam of sunlight would break through the heavy clouds and set a patch of water shimmering, each dazzling drop reflecting the light like a thousand shards of broken glass, and then all would fade once more to a dull and brooding grey.

The day brightened as the morning wore on, the sun came out, and cloud shadows moved across the green and purple mountain slopes on the far side of the loch.

The knot in my stomach loosened and the anxiety of the last few months began to dissipate as I breathed a little deeper, inhaling the sea air, the rich smell of dying bracken and wind-burnt heather, drinking in the exquisite landscape around me. This was the dream! Raw, beautiful and wild. I felt alive! Suddenly I was excited about what lay ahead. I could do this.

10

Annie and Sweeney

'They're lovely, but mad as a box of frogs. She used to be a Playboy Bunny and he's quite a bit younger than her. They're really special people, but just take them as you find them.' Stacie hung up.

We had met Stacie MacDonald in Bonar Bridge a few days earlier when we'd stopped at the shop to stock up on dog food. She had horses and dreamt of one day doing a long ride herself. She had kindly offered to help us with stops, vets and farriers while we were in the area, so, needing a day off, I had rung her to see if she could help find us somewhere to stay for two nights near Cannich.

True to her word, Stacie had indeed found us somewhere to stay, but suddenly I wasn't quite so sure. What was I letting myself in for?

After a beautiful day wandering across deserted mountains, we eventually arrived at a little single-storey cottage on the road just outside Cannich. Sweeney came out to meet us.

He was a stocky man in his late forties with a short, thick neck, a wide, flat nose and shaved head. He had a heavy London accent that sounded harsh and out of place here among the soft, musical accents of the Highlands, and his dark skin betrayed his middle-eastern heritage.

Sweeney pointed to the enormous field beyond the house that stretched away, boundless, to the distant river and said I could let

Taliesin loose among the sheep and cows that were grazing there. Taliesin ambled off to check out his new companions without so much as a backward glance and spent the whole of his day off avoiding me, the faithless creature.

I set to work sorting out my gear and setting up the tent, and all the while Sweeney chatted away to me.

It turned out that the field was not actually his. It belonged to a local farmer who had said they could use it whenever they liked. I rather doubted that the farmer had meant they could let someone camp in it with a horse and wolf for two nights, but sometimes it's best not to question these things!

Sweeney was loud, hyper, and intense. He talked a lot, hopping from one topic to the next without once pausing for breath. It was hard keeping up with his volley of impassioned words and by the end of that first half hour, I was sure I knew his entire life story and most of Annie's, too, even though I hadn't met her yet. But for all his intensity, he had a ready laugh, a nice smile, and a big heart.

When he went back indoors, a serene silence fell as I cooked a hasty dinner in the gathering dusk and then collapsed for the night.

In the morning, leaving Spirit asleep in the tent, I went in search of my hosts for the coffee and shower Sweeney had promised me.

Outside, the house was something of a building site, where Sweeney was enthusiastically working on about ten different unfinished projects all at once, bouncing from one to the other at a dizzying rate, doing a little bit on this, and a little bit on that. His work, it seemed, was as chaotic as his conversation.

Inside, the cottage was a one bedroomed affair, with an open plan kitchen and living room. There was a large open fireplace at one end and a fully decorated Christmas tree stood in the corner, which Sweeney said they left up all year round, along with the fairy lights draped across the beams so they could have the joy of Christmas every day - even though he had been raised a Muslim.

The promised coffee was almost forgotten in his boyish excitement to give me the full tour of the place while he told me about all the improvements he wanted to make to this feature or that, and what he wanted to build next. He was so excited he could barely hold a thought for more than a few seconds before he moved on to the next one, each idea changing and evolving as he spoke about it with unwavering enthusiasm and animation. It was thoroughly captivating, and more than a little exhausting.

Finally, feeling somewhat overwhelmed, I was ushered over to the sofa with the long awaited cup of coffee. There, reclining sedately in a skimpy little nightdress that left very little to the imagination, puffing away at a cigarette and watching re-runs of the X-factor on the enormous screen that nearly covered an entire wall, was Annie.

She must have been seventy if she was a day, with bleached blond hair that fell in straggling waves below her shoulders, and she had a deep gravelly voice from years of smoking. There was something very sweet and almost childlike about her, and she, like Sweeney, had a big heart.

I sat and chatted with Annie, while Sweeney bounced in and out of the house doing bits and bobs, stopping for a few seconds to join in the conversation and smoke half a cigarette before leaping up to go off and do something else. And all the while, amidst all the chaos, Annie reclined sedately in her cloud of smoke.

The whole thing was rather surreal and tripped me out no end, because after days of making our calm, quiet way through the still and silent landscape, this whirlwind of intense hyperactivity seemed utterly alien and bizarre to me. After my shower I went and lay down.

That evening I was invited in for dinner. Sweeney cooked. It was a veritable feast of roasted vegetables and salad, which I ate until I could barely move, and the alcohol flowed freely.

Sweeney was drinking beer; with each swig he became more intense and his unstoppable torrent of words became even louder and more chaotic. Annie, who was knocking back vodka on the rocks, also became louder as she tried – unsuccessfully - to get a word in edgeways. The T.V., still playing X-Factor re-runs, became increasingly louder as well, and my head began to spin - not so much from the gin and tonic I'd been drinking, but from the surreality and the chaos of it all.

The atmosphere grew more and more uncomfortable, so at last I crept away to the quiet solitude of my tent and fell into a deep sleep, glad that I would be back on the road again in the morning.

Stacie was right, they were mad as a box of frogs, but they were truly special people.

11

Fort Augustus and the
Corrieyairack Pass

It was a wet and dreary day. A light rain was falling, and ghostly tendrils of mist snaked their way through the tops of the evergreen trees on the far side of the valley as we left Cannich heading for the high hills once more.

We stopped a van on the road to ask directions because I'd not been paying attention and had become disconcertingly disorientated. The bald-headed, bearded man behind the wheel looked vaguely familiar. It took me a few minutes to realise that he was the man we had met back at the riding centre near Dingwall several days before. He asked how I had fared with 'The Dragon', and was not in the least bit surprised to learn that she hadn't been particularly forthcoming with either help or kindness. He, on the other hand, was, and he pointed out where we were on the map and gave us onward directions to Tomich.

We climbed and climbed, the roads gradually petering out to stony forest tracks just beyond the picturesque little village of Tomich, whose single street was lined with old-fashioned gas lamps. Turning off the 'main road', we followed more tracks up into the mountains under lines of marching pylons, which emerged eerily from the mist like huge metal giants, buzzing and crackling in the cold, steady drizzle that was falling.

I had the distinct impression that we were missing out on some rather spectacular views, but the weather couldn't be nice all the time and so far we'd been pretty lucky.

After a long day's journey over huge mountains and through deep valleys, we came at last to the outskirts of Fort Augustus on the shores of Loch Ness.

I stopped at the first house we came to, eagerly eyeing up the field full of lush grass below it. There was no-one home, but half a mile down the road we met a man with a wolf who, it transpired, was the owner of the house. He didn't own the field, but he knew the man who did, and after making a few phone-calls he obtained permission for us to camp.

I never got his name, but he told me he worked as a skipper on a boat on Loch Ness.

'Have you seen the monster?' I asked hopefully.

'Not since the Mrs left,' he replied with a wry grin, and I laughed.

The field was in a valley full of trees, long grass and blood-thirsty midges; so, leaving Taliesin to fend for himself, I took refuge in a mouse-infested caravan because between mice and midges, mice definitely make for better bed-fellows.

From Fort Augustus we made for the open hills again, following tracks under yet more power lines, climbing steadily up to the Corrieyairack Pass. It was steep and stony going, and as usual I found myself leading Taliesin because somehow it felt nicer than riding him. The whole way the packs, in spite of my meticulous balancing that morning, kept slipping over to one side and pulling the saddle off-centre, so we had to stop every few hundred yards and readjust the lot to absolutely no avail, which made me very grumpy indeed.

By early afternoon, the clouds, which had hung low and heavy all morning, vanished as we crested the pass and began our long descent into the valley opening up below us; wide and green, dotted here and there with large patches of dark forestry. The brown and purple mountains across the valley rolled away in every direction, ridge upon ridge across the vast and silent horizons as far as the eye could see, and a fast-flowing stream ran alongside us rushing and tumbling as it carved its path down the valley to converge with the river Spey, before making its way towards the distant sea.

I looked up as we picked our way among the huge rocks that lay strewn across the path and there, not a hundred yards above us, standing poised and majestic on a rocky outcrop, was a great antlered stag. He watched our approach, unmoving, like a silent sentinel guarding the threshold into the valley below.

There are moments in life that touch your soul; moments out of time that can be as simple as watching a bird circling in the distant light of a falling sunbeam, a shooting star burning a bright path across the night sky, or the wind that lifts a cluster of fallen autumn leaves in a swirling dance of fiery colour. Those moments are fleeting, yet captivating. Time stands still and you feel as small and insignificant as a grain of sand in the grand scheme of the universe, yet at the same time as large and expansive as the whole of the universe itself. And in those extreme yet simultaneous opposites, you can feel, for just an instant, barely tangible beyond the normal senses, the inter-connected web of all life, held in an intricate and delicate balance, stretching away across time.

Those brief moments are the most profound and intoxicating experiences of life, of beauty and of nature, nourishing the soul and bringing meaning to existence. Those are the kind of experiences that evoke feelings and an innate awareness that no words can ever fully describe. Such moments are best absorbed and savoured alone and in silence.

This was such a moment. It was pure magic. My heart soared.

12

A Slight Mishap

My stomach hit the floor.

It was gone.

I checked and rechecked, hoping against hope that my eyes were deceiving me, but the pack was definitely not there.

Before we left Cornwall, I had bought Spirit a little backpack so she could carry her own food on the journey. I had thought it a great idea, but she hadn't. She hated it and I rather suspected that it was a major contributing factor to her not really enjoying the adventure so far.

I was in a good mood that morning and, feeling kindly toward my patient and long-suffering four-legged companions, I had decided to give them both an easy day. I was leading Taliesin with the packs fixed onto the seat of my Australian stock saddle rather than behind it, in order to give his back a rest, and Spirit's little pack I had casually slung over the horn of the saddle as we set off away from Melgarve Bothy down the long road towards Glenshero Lodge.

The pack had fallen once as we were manoeuvring a gate by the lodge, at the start of a stony track leading through Glen Shirra to Loch Laggan, and I thought briefly that perhaps I ought to tie it onto the saddle in case we lost it again. But the thought was fleeting, my mind wandered, and I forgot all about it.

The going was easy, the path fairly level and after several miles, as we rounded a bend, a stunning vista opened up before us. Below lay

Loch Laggan, still and silver under rainless grey skies, nestled beneath huge, rugged mountains and on the far shore, with its many gables and tall turrets peeking out from amidst the sea of dark evergreen forest, stood Ardverikie Castle. The whole scene was breathtaking and magical, like something out of a fairy tale, and I drank in all its wild and splendid beauty.

It seemed to me that each valley we came to was different than the last. The shape and character of the mountains was ever changing, and each place appeared more beautiful than the one we had left behind. The mountains, that had been vast and rolling further north, spreading out across empty expanses of gently rising moorland, had gradually become more condensed as though the land had been pushed in from the edges to form great folds in the earth's surface - folds which in turn had been shaped and sculpted into rough forms and faces by the fierce winds, relentless rains, and the harsh ice of many long Highland winters.

So absorbed had I been in taking in my surroundings, that I had failed to notice the pack, containing all the food Spirit needed for the next two or three days, had fallen.

I looked back at the track that stretched for miles behind us, hoping I'd see the pack lying on the verge nearby. Perhaps it had fallen off when Taliesin snatched at a clump of grass a hundred yards back…? But it hadn't.

Leaving Taliesin to graze on a small grassy mound, I set off at a steady trot back the way we had come in search of the missing food, with Spirit running along beside me. We scoured every inch of ground for a good half a mile or more, and not a sign of it could be seen. I kept telling myself that it must be around the next bend, over the next small rise, but it wasn't. Eventually, I had to admit defeat and we headed back to Taliesin who nickered softly and gave me a deeply reproachful look for abandoning him there, alone, in the middle of nowhere.

To make matters worse, Spirit was suddenly, and inexplicably, limping.

The joy I had found in the beauty of my surroundings earlier that day was rapidly vanishing now as we continued on down towards the road, which ran along the northern edge of the loch. There we found our way barred by an enormous padlocked gate, with solid six-foot high fencing on either side. Just what we needed!

I was starting to spiral into a thoroughly bad mood when I suddenly noticed a little wooden access gate over to our left, across a small patch of bog. After undoing a strand of wire across the top of the gateway, and scrambling through a deep ditch, we found ourselves at last on tarmac. A short while later, just as I was wondering what on earth we were going to do about feeding poor old Spirit, help arrived in the form of two young men driving a trailer-load of food to a youth camp somewhere further up the valley.

Having passed us on the road, they pulled into a lay-by a little further ahead to talk to us about what we were doing and to offer us all some lunch, which consisted of olives, rye-bread and crisps. Spirit didn't care for any of it and lay on the tarmac looking sullen and fed up, but Taliesin and I thoroughly enjoyed our meal.

When my new friends heard about our misadventure with the dog food, they lost no time in diving into the trailer, riffling through their extensive supplies, and finally emerged bearing tins of tuna, mackerel, and sardines, along with several packets of oatcakes.

Thanks to that chance encounter, and to the generosity of those two kind men, Spirit ate like a queen for the next few days.

I was starting to relax and enjoy the journey now the crippling anxiety and terror that I had initially felt were wearing off.

We were settling into the daily rhythms of life on the road, the slow miles that were broken up by Taliesin's steady, rhythmic hoof-beats, interrupted only by frequent stops to let him graze on the verges, chat to curious passers-by, or to take in the beautiful scenery that surrounded us on every side. I was happy. I could breathe. This was freedom!

I was gaining confidence, learning to trust myself, my instincts, and my animals. Most of all I was learning to believe in the inherent goodness of my fellow humans. The only thing that really worried me now was finding somewhere to stop at the end of each day. I wasn't keen on wild camping in case Taliesin broke loose in the night and disappeared, so finding a well-fenced field had become my main, anxiety-provoking priority.

Physically the journey was proving tough, too. My whole body ached from walking and riding so many miles each day, my arms hurt from Spirit's incessant pulling, and my toes were a raw mess of painful blisters that I kept permanently wrapped up in surgical tape to alleviate some of the constant discomfort.

Wet feet were fast becoming an accepted fact of life, which probably didn't help with the blisters. My boots might occasionally dry out overnight if I was lucky, but they would be wet again within the first few miles of each day's journey from crossing streams and bogs, or simply from walking through wet grass to catch Taliesin in the morning before we even set off. More often than not, my boots and socks would not dry out over night at all and I'd start out with sodden feet, and so they would remain until the end of the day when I would peel my socks off to let them breathe for a while before it began all over again in the morning. Strangely, none of that really bothered me. It is amazing what you can tolerate when your dreams are being realised!

Even Taliesin appeared to be enjoying the journey now. He seemed to have finally stopped committing acts of protest and wanton self-destruction and was getting into the swing of things, accepting life as it came without argument. He was content to wander the hills in his usual half-dazed state, taking the world in his slow, yet ground-covering stride, with an air of easy, philosophical contemplation, and eating whenever the opportunity arose. There was no doubt that I had chosen the right horse for the job!

Only Spirit remained unconvinced.

She had been pretty miserable for the last few days, lying down, looking dejectedly at me with her sad brown eyes and whining whenever I stopped to consult the map or let Taliesin graze. She was tired and her paws were starting to become sore from all the rough terrain we were covering, but she objected to having to wear boots to protect her pads. She was definitely missing her comparatively lazy life of luxury back home in Cornwall, where the majority of our daily miles were covered swiftly in my little blue van, and a 'walk' usually meant a little two or three mile stroll around the block, rather than twenty-three miles of hard slog over rocky mountain tracks. At the end of these hikes, tired and aching, instead of a nice comfy bed to sleep on she was given smelly, sweat-soaked horse blankets in a tent that still reeked of rotting midges. Well it just wasn't good enough!

I offered her little sympathy in her sulks though, and told her that her sense of adventure left a lot to be desired. You would think she'd have loved being out on the move with her pack, exploring new territory all day long, and yet of the three of us she had the most misgivings!

13

Be Careful What You Wish For

We were soaked to the bone and freezing cold, high up in the hills heading for the shores of Loch Ossian. It was the first time in fourteen days of travelling across the Scottish Highlands that we'd encountered anything more than a light rain. That must be a record for Scotland, so we had nothing to complain about really, but it was miserable all the same. Utterly so.

The mountains were lagged in low cloud and I could see very little of my surroundings. The heavy rain, accompanied by a biting and relentless wind, was finding its way in under my not-so-waterproof jacket. Cold rain soaked up along the lining of the sleeves and down the neck of my coat until no part of the hoodie I wore underneath remained dry. My water-proof trousers had given up any claim to that title a long time ago so my legs, too, were soaked. I walked with my animals in an effort to warm myself up, feet squelching in water-logged boots, but nothing seemed to ward off the cold. I was frozen through.

The only good thing about the day was that Spirit seemed to be slightly less lame and her mood had improved now she didn't have to carry any packs. She was almost beginning to enjoy the journey! She trotted happily along beside us, gleefully chasing the sticks I threw for her and following little scent-trails through the boggy terrain that bordered the rough and stony track.

Eventually, failing to warm up or thaw out and feeling pretty fed up, I climbed into the saddle and Taliesin carried me gently and without complaint through the grounds of Courour Lodge, tucked high up in the hills, many miles from anywhere. Leaving the shores of Loch Ossian behind us, we climbed higher into the hills, where the wind picked up and blew more cold rain into my face and down my neck, before beginning a slow and steady descent towards Loch Rannoch.

I sat huddled and shivering in the saddle, head bent against the driving rain, wallowing in self-pity and dreading having to spend the night in a wet tent. I prayed desperately for some kind, beautiful souls to take pity on me and offer me somewhere warm to sleep where I could thaw out and dry my sodden clothes.

And we found it!

When we reached Bridge of Gaur at the head of Loch Rannoch, a kind woman named Mary offered me and Spirit a warm, dry shed to sleep in and she let me sit in by the fire with a hot cup of tea while my clothes steamed away in front of the Aga. Taliesin, however, was left in a paddock where there was not a decent blade of grass to be found, next door to Mary's overweight Exmoor pony.

'There's plenty of grass there!' Mary assured me. 'It's been rested for a week!'

Taliesin didn't think so. He didn't even try to put his head down to graze and just stood looking at me expectantly as I walked away to the warm, dry house.

I knew the paddock wasn't good enough for Taliesin, who had carried me so faithfully for the best part of thirty miles over the cold, wet mountains. I knew I should have pushed on in search of better grazing for him because he needed it that day, and every day on the journey, but I didn't like to be rude to Mary who had been good enough to offer us a place for the night - and the promise of somewhere warm to sleep where I could dry my clothes was too much of a temptation for me. I had spent the day desperately wishing for this, and that wish had been granted. So I sacrificed Taliesin's well-being for my own comfort that night.

57

In the morning, feeling warm, dry and well-rested, I went out to find Taliesin, cold, hungry and tucked up, and all along his back were hot, hard lumps where either the saddle had rubbed him the day before when he'd so faithfully carried me all those cold, wet miles, or where the insects had feasted on him that night while he went hungry. To add to all of that, he had a sore coming up on his side where the girth had rubbed him.

I have never felt so guilty in all my life and I swear that never again, until the day I die, will I ever put my own selfish desires before the needs of my horse. It was a bad move and I am not proud of my choices that day.

I didn't ride when we set off again because I was worried about the saddle rubbing and turning the lumps into open sores. I kept the girth a bit looser, too, in a futile attempt to avoid aggravating the girth gall, and we stopped often so Taliesin could graze on the best grass we could find to make up for what he had missed the night before, and to appease my guilty conscience.

We hugged the shoreline of Loch Rannoch for several miles, following a road that wound through large patches of native woodland. Then, leaving the road and the moody waters of the loch behind us, we climbed up into the Tay Forest Park, making our silent way beneath the dark, evergreen trees, along earthen tracks that were carpeted in a thick layer of sweet-smelling pine needles. Emerging finally onto the open hillsides, we followed the course of a stream as we dropped steadily and steeply down into the beautiful Glen Lyon.

We stayed for two nights at a Bed and Breakfast at Bridge of Balgie where Taliesin rested, feasting on rich grass and gazing adoringly at the small herd of cows in the adjacent field. I feasted, too, on good food and copious amounts of tea, and I spent a day exploring the valley; wandering along river banks and among the little cattle-grazed knolls on which birch and alder trees grew, casting their dappled shade onto the soft green grass and yellow mosses of that beautiful fairy glen.

When we left Glen Lyon the silent mountains were once again hidden behind a heavy curtain of low cloud that soon turned to a steady rain.

The narrow road climbed for several miles, following a wide gulley between the barren hills, and then levelled out as it skirted the shores of Lochan Na Lairige. At the far end of the loch, the dark shape of Lawlers Dam towered, ghostly in the trailing mist, and beyond it the road dropped gently down again towards gloomy Loch Tay.

Upon reaching the busy main road that led into Killin, the heavens opened, rain bucketed down, and by the time we reached the town and began asking around for somewhere to stop, we were soaked through and thoroughly fed up.

I was leading Taliesin again that day. The lumps on his back had gone down significantly but he still had a few just behind the saddle where the packs would normally sit, so I'd fixed the packs onto the saddle to save his back and had walked.

As we trudged wearily through Killin, splashing along in the streams of water that came gushing down the road, our heads bent against the driving rain and feeling quite wet and miserable, I suddenly noticed a sign advertising an outdoor clothing sale happening that very day in the village hall. I desperately needed new waterproofs and who knew when I'd next have the chance to replace them. The timing was perfect!

Arriving at the village hall, I hitched the animals up to a parking meter outside and went in search of some new, and not too expensive, replacements for my tattered and useless waterproofs. I found some! Not only that, but I also got chatting to a man who rang round a bunch of people, who in turn rang a few more, and the next thing we knew we were heading out of Killin looking for Acharn Lodges, where the owner, a kind old Swede called Rolf, and his lovely wife, Celia, offered us some warm hospitality for the night.

First, Taliesin was turned out into an enormous field of good grass with Rolf's elderly Arabian gelding, Halim, who was spoilt rotten and totally revered by his doting owner. I was a little apprehensive about letting the two horses run loose together in case Taliesin took a dislike to Halim and tried to run him through a fence, as he had been known to do with other horses in the past, or else delivered a blow to this wisp of a horse with one of his enormous iron-clad feet. But, to my great relief, Taliesin behaved with the utmost decorum, and was polite and well mannered towards his host. In fact, he was more interested in scratching his enormous backside against the tall oak trees that grew around the paddock than he was in his companion!

Then, with Taliesin settled, to my utter surprise and delight, I was offered an empty holiday let for the night where there was a clean, comfortable bed to sleep in, a hot bath to soak in, and somewhere warm to dry my sodden clothes. This unexpected kindness was both delightful and humbling!

I passed a splendid evening with my warm-hearted and generous hosts, and that night as I fell asleep listening to the rain pounding on the skylight above my bed, I was grateful to be inside and dry. I was even more grateful that Taliesin had some good grazing, a stable to shelter in, and some company for the night, too.

14

Jack Black

For the first time on the journey I was worried. There was something about the man that made me uneasy. He was too hyper, too unpredictable, too ... wired! I really wasn't comfortable with the idea that he knew where I was camped, that it was an isolated spot, and that I was on my own. What made me even more uncomfortable still was that he'd said he would come up and see me that evening.

Taliesin, Spirit, and I had spent the day wandering along an almost deserted cycle path from Killin to Callander. The track, which was wide, flat, and well paved, ran parallel to the busy main road on the opposite side of Glen Ogle. Passing the head of Loch Earn, the trail dropped gently down and then levelled out beyond the mouth of Blaquidder Glen, whose hills stretched away into the distance to our right. We followed the course of a river through Strathyre and then into thick conifer forests where eventually, after many quiet miles, we emerged in the middle of a busy complex of holiday lodges on the shores of Loch Lubnaig.

Stopping at the cafe there, I left my animals tied up to some railings outside and headed in to get a drink and to chat to the staff about finding somewhere to camp for the night. A pleasant man named Tom agreed to help us in exchange for a photograph of our little fellowship. True to his word, in the time it took me to polish off a cold drink and talk to some of the curious holidaymakers and members of staff, Tom managed to obtain permission for us to camp in an old burial ground just outside Callander.

When I returned to my animals with Tom for the promised photograph, we found Jack, the forest ranger, taking pictures of himself with Taliesin and Spirit. He was dressed in green, and wore a beret with a feather sticking out at a jaunty angle. He must have been somewhere in his sixties, was short and stocky, with close-cropped grey hair; he had a round boyish face, red cheeks, and a hyper enthusiasm that reminded me somewhat of Sweeney back in Cannich.

Jack had worked with horses in the army, he told me, carrying supplies and explosives through the jungle where he'd been posted. One day, he'd like to walk around Scotland with a pack pony. He'd pop up to the cemetery and see me later on that evening, he said, when Tom told him where we were camping. He wanted to see my set up, have a look at my equipment, and pick my brains for when he did something similar himself.

My heart sank.

On the surface he seemed a nice enough guy. Nothing he said gave me good reason to be worried by him. Nevertheless, I didn't like the fact he knew where I'd be camping, that I was alone, and that it was an isolated spot. And I certainly didn't want him coming up there. But I couldn't think of a good reason to tell him not to without sounding rude.

The panic was rising. For the first time in nearly three weeks of wild camping and staying with total strangers, I felt vulnerable and scared. All the stark warnings people had given me before I set off about the dangers of a woman travelling alone came flooding back, and every brutal horror story I had ever read about solo female travellers, campers or hitch-hikers, flashed through my mind in one terrifying show-reel of violent possibility. I thought about pushing on, finding somewhere else to stop for the night, a place where I couldn't be found by this man, but most of the surrounding landscape was forested and there weren't many fields. What if I didn't find anything? We had covered enough miles that day, and we really needed to stop.

Surely I was just being paranoid and letting my imagination run away with me; this man wasn't a threat.

All the same, I was worried.

As we left the holiday park, squeezing through a narrow gate alongside a cattle grid, Spirit suddenly stopped to sniff something. Taliesin, who as usual was lost in his own little world and only half aware of what was happening around him, didn't notice and stepped straight onto her hind paw with one of his enormous hooves. He then stopped dead, pinning her to the ground, to see what all the fuss was about as she let out a series of heart-rending yelps. It took a few seconds for him to get going again, because there is always a delay while things register with Taliesin, and when he finally shifted his weight off the traumatised dog he left behind him a great bleeding gash, right across one of her toes.

This day was getting progressively worse.

Poor old Spirit! It was a wonder he'd not cut her toe clean off, or worse, her whole paw! Yet by some miracle, she wasn't even limping, although the cut was bleeding badly.

There's a strong argument for not taking a dog on a journey like this. It's a big responsibility and adds a whole load of stress and worry to your existing daily problems. Firstly, they can be a liability with other dogs and livestock (Spirit certainly was!), which can make finding places to stop more difficult; secondly, if they get injured, which is pretty likely to happen at some point, it can mess up the whole adventure and cause long, expensive delays; and thirdly, not only do you have to source and carry food for yourself and possibly your horse, but you also have to source and carry food for the dog, which many would argue adds unnecessary weight to the horse's load.

But, for all of that, she was a good companion, and I'd not willingly have left her behind.

We found the burial ground, a small mound rising up out of a big, level floodplain where cows and sheep roamed freely. It was right at the junction of two rivers and there were old, toppling headstones scattered about the hill under tall and ancient trees next to the remains of an old chapel.

The mound was fenced off from the surrounding plain with some rusty, iron-rail fencing which was falling down in several places, but once reinforced with some of the electric fencing I carried, it made a decent enough paddock for Taliesin with ample grazing for the night.

I set about making camp on top of the hill among the gravestones where the ground was flat and washed out the gash on Spirit's paw with some disinfectant, before trying to wrap a bandage around it to keep it clean. She gave me a resentful look and within a few minutes had pulled the bandage off, so I gave up and put some cream on her paw instead, which she managed to smear all over the inside of the tent, my sleeping bag, and the saddle blankets that made up her bed.

I was just settling down to my dinner when Spirit began to growl. Looking up I saw Jack clambering over the rusty railings at the foot of the knoll. He looked taken aback at Spirit's greeting. She had been friendly towards him at the lodges earlier on - but it's one thing meeting someone on neutral territory during the day, and quite another when that someone was coming into our camp at night. Spirit knew the difference. If I'd had any misgivings at all about having her along on the journey, they vanished now. She was a good guard dog and her instincts were spot on.

Jack approached with caution, warily eyeing up the still growling Spirit. I made no attempt to stop her.

He sat down on a rock nearby, took off his rucksack, and proceeded to take out of it a whole load of supplies: oatcakes, energy bars, and porridge pots to help us on our way, and some fine Scottish whiskey, should I want a nightcap. After half an hour or so chatting about all the pros and cons and the ups and downs of horseback travel, Jack slung his now empty rucksack over his shoulder, hopped over the rusting fence, and I watched as he made his way across the plain into the fading light, the feather in his cap bobbing merrily with each step.

I breathed a sigh of relief. I had been wrong about him. Thank goodness.

In the morning, we stopped at a cafe in the town square in Callander that Jack had recommended to me, and because he'd told everyone in that small town about us, I was given a free coffee and a hearty breakfast to set me up for a long day walking through the hills. I felt very guilty then for being so mistrustful of that funny little man.

15

The Lowlands

Leaving Callander, we made our way along the shores of Loch Venachar then up over the last ridge of Highland mountains, following a cycle path which brought us out eventually at Aberfoyle. From there the land stretched away dull, and flat, for miles and miles to the south. Not that we could see much of it through the sheets of pouring rain!

I was in low spirits that day, not just because of the miserable weather and my injured wolf, but also because I was now worried about Taliesin.

As well as the smattering of lumps and bumps under his saddle, Taliesin was starting to look thin. I'd noticed that morning whilst getting him tacked up that his thighs were looking hollow and his hip bones beginning to protrude.

When we had set off nearly three weeks earlier the grass had still been quite rich, but it was mid-September now, autumn was setting in and the rough grass up in the mountains no longer had the goodness Taliesin needed to sustain him. I'd always struggled to keep the weight on him at the best of times, but the stress of being on the road really wasn't helping.

On the surface, Taliesin seemed calm and relaxed, taking each day as it came without objection, but horses are herd animals - they need the company of other equines to feel happy and secure. A lone horse can't switch off, can't relax; he'll always be alert, listening out for danger, unable to get the sleep or the rest that he needs. Between that and the poor quality of the grass, it was little wonder that Taliesin was losing weight!

I did what I could and increased the time Taliesin spent grazing each day. I took more frequent days off, tried to ask less of him, and I accepted the offer of feed whenever possible. But it was a losing battle, as once gone, the weight was near impossible to regain. The best I could hope for was to maintain his condition and try to ensure he didn't lose any more weight, but we weren't even a third of the way yet! Still, at least the grass down here off the mountains was richer.

In the lowlands we picked up a section of the Rob Roy Way, a long distance trail named after the eighteenth century Scottish folk hero and outlaw, Rob Roy MacGregor. Some say he's Scotland's answer to Robin Hood, but in less romanticised accounts, he appears to have been little more than a cattle rustler, a bully, and an all round crook.

As we approached Drymen, we had a chance encounter with Dixe Wills - a travel writer, comedian and journalist - who was walking the Rob Roy Way for an article he was going to write. Dixe possessed an uncanny ability to spot a fellow vegan from a mile off. Quite how he had sussed my dietary ilk, I could not fathom. It wasn't as though I fitted that old, and quite inaccurate, stereotype of being pale and malnourished, with a half-starved look. Far from it!

We stopped to pass the time of day. Dixe had a dry, somewhat sarcastic sense of humour, and after a short prelude, he tried to get one up on me by informing me with an air of grave superiority that he had been vegan for all of nine years. None of this trendy, band-waggoning veganism for Dixe! He was an original specimen!

Unimpressed by this implied slight on my dietary authenticity, I shamelessly pulled vegan rank, and pointed out that I out-veganed him by at least three years. Although Dixe looked a little crestfallen, he conceded defeat because, in light of the facts, I quite clearly had more right to feel smug and superior than he did.

With those very important issues safely out of the way, and our pecking order firmly established, some rather jocular conversation ensued and commiserations were exchanged on years of being dished up steamed vegetables and a dressing-less side salad in restaurants, maybe with some rice if we were lucky - but only if the chef was going all out! These up-start millennial vegans with their fancy almond milk lattes, seitan burgers, and hummus wraps from popular food outlets all across the country really had no idea what we long-suffering pioneers had endured before veganism became fashionable! When Dixe and I parted ways it was with a feeling of mutual solidarity, with the world put very much to rights, firmly united in our sense of justified superiority over just about everyone.

People often asked me if being vegan on the road was difficult and I can't say that it was. Explaining my dietary ethics to hosts - particularly if they were farmers, deer-stalkers, or the like - could be a little awkward at times, but generally we respected each other's views and got along perfectly peaceably because neither party tried to tell the other that they were wrong in their beliefs and moral values. And that, dear people, is the secret to a quiet and peaceful life.

In Drymen, after a short stop at the Co-op where I treated us all to oatcakes, carrots, and some hummus - which Taliesin spat out in disgust - we picked up the West Highland Way. It was a busy long distance path, which was overrun with hordes of walkers and strings of cyclists, out of whose way we had to constantly dodge - no mean feat on the narrow, puddle-strewn track with a wide draught horse and saddle bags to boot! And there were an awful lot of gates, too.

Since her accident, Spirit had developed a strong aversion to gates. It seemed that she associated them with being trodden on, rather than her irritating habit of stopping dead in the middle of the path to sniff something. And so, she carried on stopping dead in the middle of the path to sniff things, oblivious to how narrowly she avoided being trodden on again on a multitude of occasions, but whenever we reached a gate - which on that leg of our journey was about once every half a mile or so - she would get all in a tizz and charge through the gate at top speed as soon as it was open a crack, running right to the end of the lead, and yanking my arm half out of its socket in the process.

While Spirit had made it her goal to get through the gates as fast as possible, Taliesin, on the other hand, had decided that pausing at gates while I went about opening them was a good opportunity to put his head down to graze. Needless to say, the going along that stretch was incredibly slow, and more than a little irritating.

We were approaching Glasgow now, and suddenly there were more roads, more traffic and more people. It was civilisation: loud, crowded, and rushing. This litter-strewn jungle of tarmac, bricks, and mortar was an unpleasant shock to the senses after all those weeks of wandering in quiet solitude through silent mountains, where the only noise was the call of the wild birds, the sound of rushing water, or the wind stirring the heather on hillsides where cloud shadows shifted in ever changing patterns of light, and all was reflected in the pensive waters of deep mountain lochs.

But in amongst the creeping suburbs of the city with all the chaos, noise and grime, we found little havens where kind strangers took us in and gave us all shelter for the night. By meeting people like that, you learn to believe in the goodness of human nature and people's willingness to offer help and hospitality - not because they want something in return, but simply because it is theirs to give, and they choose to offer it freely.

16

The Question of Shoes

'What do you do about shoes?' It was a question asked by every horse owner we met on our travels, and it was a valid one.

As we came down off the mountains, it became apparent that Taliesin urgently needed new shoes. The clips on the toes of his front shoes had fallen off a few days earlier, and what was left underneath was rapidly disintegrating. I needed a farrier, and soon. But, as most equestrians will know, getting hold of one is no mean feat.

They're a pretty elusive breed, farriers, who rarely answer their phones, never respond to messages and if, by some miracle, you do manage to get hold of one, it's unlikely he'll want to come out and shoe your horse at short notice, especially if you're not a regular customer. If I could possibly help it, I'd not bother with them - the shoes or the farriers!

I'm actually not a great fan of nailing bits of metal onto horses' feet and have never really gone in for it, except when doing long rides. I think it's an expensive, and fairly unnecessary, practice for the majority of equines, who are barely ridden more than a few miles a week, and I personally don't believe it does a horse much good as it stops the hoof from functioning as it was designed to. But then horses weren't really designed to be ridden, and certainly not for hundreds of miles over abrasive surfaces, carrying a rider and a load of camping equipment, so somewhere down the line you have to compromise on these things or you'll end up in quite a fix half way up a mountain in the back of beyond, with a lame horse.

'What about hoof-boots?' I can already hear the accusatory cries emanating from the barefoot camp. Well, I'm all for them in theory, but not so much in practice.

I had only ever found one company that made hoof-boots large enough for my shaggy old lump of a draught horse, and sadly those just couldn't withstand his constant tripping, stumbling, and general bashing about, thus requiring costly and time-consuming repairs nearly every other day. And that was at home, where we were doing relatively short rides! I wasn't willing to spend forty-five minutes fiddling about with a screwdriver, replacing gaiters, wires, and clips, half way up a mountain in the pouring rain every time Taliesin broke something; nor was I prepared to carry all the spare parts I would need for such an undertaking. There just wasn't room in my saddlebags.

No, I had decided, we'd have to try our luck with the farriers!

I'd had Taliesin shod before we left Cornwall, and since leaving Durness, we'd covered nearly 350 miles, which I didn't think was bad going - although, judging by the state of the shoes, I'd had my money's worth out of them.

Because Taliesin has incredibly good, hard feet, I had decided to leave his hind hooves unshod when we set off, to see how far we could get. It had soon become apparent that his feet were no match for the rough, stony tracks of the Scottish Highlands, and a week into the journey I'd had to admit to making a very silly mistake. I rang five of the nine registered farriers in the area, leaving messages for all of them, and as usual, not a single one had bothered to reply. In the end I had once again called in the help of Stacie MacDonald. True to her promise, she had helped me find a farrier, who came out to us at Cannich and put the two most expensive shoes I have ever come across onto Taliesin's hind feet, and without road studs either, so poor Taliesin slipped like a penguin on a glacier over every smooth surface we encountered!

When I realised that Taliesin's front shoes were now almost completely worn out, and having once again failed to get hold of a farrier, I did what I usually do and deferred the situation to Providence, in the hope that It would, as It usually did, provide.

And luckily for us, It did. We took shelter one night with Fiona of Milndavie Farm Riding Centre, and when I asked her about a blacksmith, she lost no time in ringing her own farrier and arranging for him to shoe Taliesin the following day.

The farrier turned up as promised and in no time at all, he had pulled off Taliesin's worn out front shoes. Amidst clouds of steam, the stench of burning hoof, and the clanging of metal, he shaped and fitted two new ones, road studs and all, and for less than half the price of the shoes we'd had put on back in Cannich.

Maybe farriers aren't all so bad!

17

Davy Gray

'**D**id you know Kirsty used to be a glamour model for The Sun?' Davy asked me.

I was sitting at the kitchen table drinking coffee with my hosts, the Gray family - Davy, Fiona, and their daughter, Heather. Davy was referring to the lovely woman who, several days earlier, had invited me into her home, offered me a shower, washed my clothes, and given me a bed for the night, while Taliesin filled up on good grass at the yard over the road where Kirsty kept her horses. I had spent a pleasant evening curled up on the sofa in front of a roaring fire, drinking gin and tonic with Kirsty and her daughter, Laura. A nicer, more welcoming pair of women I could not have wished to meet!

I laughed when Davy told me that, because this was coming from the man who only moments before had taken great pride in telling me how he had once made national headlines for using an inflatable sex doll as a scarecrow. The calibre of my hosts in Scotland had sunk to whole new depths! But if I was learning one thing on my journey, it was to take people as I found them and not to judge anyone save for how they treated me and my animals. Everything else was of little relevance.

'He's a bit of a comedian,' Kirsty had warned, when she phoned to say she'd found us somewhere to stay.

He certainly was that! Davy had a wicked sense of humour, didn't take life too seriously, and could turn almost anything into a joke. I liked him. He was one of those people who made you feel instantly at ease.

Fiona, too, was a cheerful, relaxed sort of person, who was never far off a smile. They were a lovely family, the Grays, for all their bizarre crow-scaring methods.

We had arrived at Glenhead Farm, where Davy reared sheep and trained working dogs, in the middle of the afternoon after an easy day spent wandering along flat cycle tracks and canal paths, slipping almost unnoticed through the busy towns where only a few people had stopped to stare. Most were too wrapped up in their hectic lives and dragged down by their own problems to notice a big, lumbering horse piled high with packs, a weary, foot-sore woman, and a little grey wolf moving quietly through the hustle and bustle of their daily existence. The leaves of the trees that lined the banks of the Forth and Clyde Canal were just beginning to turn, and the fading greens and bright yellows stood out against the blue September skies. There was a distinct bite to the air in the mornings now. Autumn was upon us.

The farm was situated at the end of a long track, half way up a hill surrounded by fields of sheep. The farmhouse was nestled in the corner of a large, concrete yard surrounded by barns and outbuildings, and opposite the house stood a row of kennels full of neurotic sheepdogs who went mad barking their heads off and leaping up at the mesh doors of their enclosures, if so much as a leaf stirred on the yard.

Davy said he could tell from the way they barked what had set them off, whether it was an escaped sheep, an unfamiliar dog, a person they knew or a stranger coming up the drive. Who needs hi-tech security systems when you can have a dozen bonkers collies instead?

After turning Taliesin out into a nice rich pasture with some sheep and a little orphaned calf for company, Davy showed me to the annex adjoining the farmhouse that he'd built for his late mother, told me I could stay there, and laughed at my look of surprise at this unexpected luxury. The most I had been hoping for was a barn!

The front door of the annex led from the yard straight into a big room that served as both a kitchen and a sitting room. A door led off this into the bedroom where there was a double bed and an en-suite bathroom. There was another door leading from the bedroom straight through into the farmhouse kitchen.

Davy was an enormous man, not fat, just tall and rather squarely built, and I think he had designed the annex to fit his own gigantic proportions because everything in it seemed to have been made for a giant. At 5'6" I don't consider myself all that short, but I was dwarfed by the interior - the enormous double bed was so high I almost had to jump to get into it; the bath (which to my absolute delight doubled up as a Jacuzzi) was the size of a small swimming pool; and my feet dangled above the floor when I sat on the loo.

'Stay as long as you like,' Davy said with a grin, after showing me around. 'It's nae bother at all.'

So we stayed for two nights, because Taliesin needed some good grass, Spirit looked like she could do with the rest, and I didn't know when I'd next see a bed again, never mind a bath. I felt I had better make the most of it while I could.

It dawned on me that, so far, I seemed to have spent more time sleeping indoors than I had spent actually sleeping in the tent. And I wasn't the least bit sorry about it either!

My day off was spent stocking up on supplies, catching up on sleep, and working out the next part of my journey. I wanted to avoid some of the bigger towns, and find the quietest route across the many motorways, main roads, and railway lines that spread out around Glasgow like the spokes of an enormous wheel.

That evening my hosts were having a party. It was Davy's birthday and a few of his friends had come round for dinner. I was invited to join them and we passed a rather jolly evening eating, drinking, and laughing a lot. Spirit disgraced herself by pouncing on Fiona's little dog for no conceivable reason and so was banished back to the annex, and I drank far too much gin, because by the time I climbed up into that enormous bed and shut my eyes, the room had started to spin.

I awoke the next morning feeling surprisingly bright and chipper, all things considered, and was up, packed and in the kitchen for breakfast by eight o'clock. I was barely half way through my second cup of coffee when the dogs in the yard started up a deafening chorus.

Looking out the window to see what the commotion was about, Davy turned to me with a mischievous grin and said:

'There's a horse in the yard.'

'Yeah, right!' I rolled my eyes. This was his idea of a joke. It was too early in the morning and I wasn't falling for it.

'I'm serious!' he said, still grinning.

Doubtfully, I got up to look, just to be sure. It took me a few seconds to realise that for once he actually wasn't pulling my leg. Taliesin was indeed wandering about in the yard among the flock of free-range chickens, checking out all the buildings, vehicles, and bits of farm machinery with great interest. He seemed totally oblivious to the ruckus his presence was causing in the kennels opposite, where a dozen sheepdogs were leaping four feet into the air and hurling themselves at the doors of their pens in a mad cacophony of barking, yelping, and howling.

Taliesin greeted me with a cheerful nicker and ambled slowly over when I emerged from the house, armed with a head collar and a carrot. Clearly he was keen to get back on the road! So much so, he had actually managed to take down a row of hurdles, letting himself and half of Davy's sheep out in his eagerness to find me and get our little party moving again. I was almost touched by this display of loyalty, and I realised that to him, Spirit and I had become his herd, the only bit of familiarity he had out here, hundreds of miles from the security of home. No wonder he didn't like days off when he hardly saw either of us!

Some of the lumps along his back had started to rub now and the hair had all but vanished in places, revealing patches of dark grey skin underneath, and giving him a rather moth-eaten appearance. To my frustration, new lumps had emerged elsewhere along his back as well. I still wasn't sure what had caused them, whether it was insect bites, a grain of dirt trapped under the saddle, or whether the saddle itself was rubbing. Whatever it was I wasn't happy about it, as the last thing we needed were open sores if the skin broke.

I hadn't ridden Taliesin since that night at Bridge of Gaur by Loch Rannoch, hoping that if I kept the weight and pressure on his back to a minimum, the lumps might go away. But so far, no such luck. So I decided to just keep on leading him and see what happened. Anyway, I quite liked walking beside him, discussing anything and everything with him, and telling him often how much I adored him. He listened to my ramblings with a deeply philosophic air, plodding amiably along, and every now and then he'd trip over one of his own hooves. Although they were the size of dinner plates, somehow he never quite seemed to know where they were.

18

Lanark

We spent another day skirting around Glasgow, slipping through the busy suburbs of outlying towns and trudging across bleak and dreary wastelands strewn with litter and wind farms. All the towns and villages we went through were grim, soulless places, which bore a general air of hopelessness. It was very gloomy and depressing. People had warned me that these were rough areas and not to wild camp if I could help it, so I had arranged for us to spend the night at Windyedge Equestrian Centre on the eastern edge of Glasgow.

I slept comfortably on the floor of the indoor arena, while Taliesin stood about getting hot and sweaty in a stable, eating hay that made him cough, until I went and ran a hose over it for him. He really doesn't do well being stabled, and it didn't help that the thick, shaggy coat he grows each autumn in preparation for the arctic winters we never get was starting to come in.

I had to refill his hay net again in the middle of the night because it was empty. I noticed that all the horses on the yard had finished their rations, too, and that would be it for them until the staff arrived the following morning. I couldn't help but think what a boring life it must be for a horse standing about in a stable for so many hours with nothing to eat and nothing to do.

Leaving Windyedge, we continued on in the direction of Lanark and the countryside became gradually more interesting again, with green pastures and rolling hills that climbed, row upon row, up towards another distant range of mountains.

A horse lorry passed us on a little back road and the men driving it stopped to chat. When they heard what we were doing, they offered us a lift to our next stop, still a good seven miles away. It was a kind offer but I felt that would be cheating, and so, as tempting as it was, I declined and trudged on.

It was late in the day when we finally arrived at our destination just south of Lanark. We had been invited to stay with Maggie and Ian that night. They were both ex-coppers from London, who had retired from the Metropolitan Police Service and moved north to enjoy the peace and tranquility of Lanarkshire.

Taliesin was put into a paddock nearby with a hearty bucket of feed and a pile of nice haylage - which the Travellers' ponies from next door broke in to share with him during the night - while Spirit and I were treated to some wonderful hospitality in the home of our lovely hosts.

I soaked my sore muscles in a steaming hot bath, tended to the open, painful blisters on my toes that had come up after so many days of walking. At last, feeling clean and semi-human again, I sat down to a scrumptious dinner with my hosts. I was very well fed, and very well watered - mostly with gin and tonic, which helped to alleviate the aches and pains of the twenty-odd miles I had walked that day. Finally, almost too tired to keep my eyes open any longer, I sank into a huge, comfortable bed and drifted into a deep sleep.

'Stay as long as you like,' Maggie and Ian offered.

In the morning, after some mild protestations, I accepted their kind invitation because even though it had only been two days since our last day off, there was no rush to get anywhere and our hosts were such warm, welcoming people that it seemed silly not to stay and enjoy their company and hospitality a while longer. After all, wasn't this what it was all about?

19

The RDA

'Are you raising money for charity?' I had been asked this on all my previous journeys by nearly everyone we met. And I hadn't been. In fact, it hadn't even occurred to me to use my dreams of horseback travel as a fundraising campaign. But it became apparent from the way people looked taken aback, and then eyed me up with deep suspicion as though I were some kind of lunatic (which in all fairness, was probably a reasonable assessment), that to most people the notion of heading off on an epic adventure purely for the sake of it was utterly unfathomable. Do such a thing in aid of a good cause, however, and suddenly everyone's all for it and cheering you on from the sidelines.

There is a nagging, purist voice in the back of my head, which stubbornly insists that one ought to be able to journey for the sheer sake of it, without having to justify or disguise it as an act of charitable kindness. But in spite of those reservations, I felt that if someone somewhere could benefit from my mad undertaking and the fulfilment of a life-long dream, then why on earth shouldn't they? And after much deliberation about which charity would be the most worthy beneficiary, it suddenly came to me: the Riding for the Disabled Association!

Founded in 1969, the Riding for the Disabled Association (RDA) is a charity that enables people with a wide range of disabilities to ride or drive horses. What began fifty years ago as a small group of able-bodied individuals with a vision of helping a few disabled people, grew and grew until now there were over five-hundred RDA groups across the UK, helping more than twenty-five thousand individuals each year.

The effect of horses on people, particularly those with disabilities, mental health, or psychological issues has long been acknowledged, and the efficacy of using horses for treatment has been well documented. In fact, there are a whole range of therapeutic techniques which fall under the umbrella term of Equine Assisted Therapy, covering anything from psychotherapy and counselling, personal growth and learning, to therapeutic riding or driving.

Therapeutic riding and driving, which are what the RDA offer, are not only recognised for improving balance, posture, core strength, and fine motor skills, but have also been shown to improve people's confidence and promote an overall sense of well-being. Using my adventure to support a charity that worked with horses to help people was perfect!

The RDA hadn't been a completely random choice, however. When I was six years old, my parents had moved to a Camphill Village Trust Community for people with special needs, where we had shared a home and lived as a family with five adults whose challenges ranged from Down syndrome, autism, and cerebral palsy, to schizophrenia and bi-polar disorder, all with learning difficulties as well. Ours was one of ten Camphill Community houses on a small estate on the outskirts of London. We had cows and goats for milk, chickens for eggs, large gardens in which the community grew food, and a bakery, woodwork shop, weavery, pottery, and basketry, where the residents in the community worked during the week. Looking back, it was a wonderful way to grow up, giving me a very different perspective on life, and helping to shape how I view the world and the people in it.

Several of the residents in the community, including three from our household, attended weekly sessions at the local RDA centre. I was able to witness first hand not just the pleasure it brought them, but the significant improvements in mobility, confidence, and general well-being, too. A few weeks spent volunteering at the centre in my holidays one summer gave me yet more experience of just what the charity brought to the lives of the people it helped, and provided greater insights into the valuable work it did in the community.

Yes, I decided, the RDA was a cause well worth supporting! It was an added bonus that it had centres all over the country, some of which fell on, or near to, my route. That opened up the possibility of having help with finding places to stop on our journey south, should we need it. In fact, that was how I ended up staying with Maggie and Ian at Lanark, because Maggie was the chairwoman for the Clydesdale RDA group and Ian was the secretary. I had emailed them before setting off, and they had been more than happy to offer us hospitality on our way through.

The Clydesdale RDA group hired ponies and a sand-school from the Scottish Equestrian Centre in Lanark a couple of days a week. On my day off, I accompanied Maggie and Ian in to watch the morning's session, which was being held for a group of local primary school children with a range of needs.

The children arrived eager and excited for their ride; docile ponies were led into the arena by volunteers, lined up at the mounting block, and the children were helped into the saddle. The session largely involved navigating small obstacle courses and playing games on horseback, interspersed with little bursts of trot here and there.

The children all thoroughly enjoyed themselves, and the difference in them on and off the ponies was extraordinary! Before their session, some were hyperactive and struggling to focus and communicate, but once mounted they were altogether different: calm, confident, and balanced, and some of the more introverted children became positively chatty. The teachers who accompanied the children told me that after their ride, the children remained calmer and more focussed in the classroom for the rest of the day.

It was amazing that something as simple as sitting on a horse could have such a profound effect in so short a period of time.

Maggie told me later that the Clydesdale RDA group was struggling not only to raise enough funds to keep the sessions running, but also to recruit volunteers to help out with the lessons. In particular, they were lacking young, able-bodied individuals to lead the horses and act as side helpers to the riders. As a result, the group simply couldn't accommodate even a fraction of the people who needed their help, which was a shame as it was clear that even a weekly half-hour session made a huge difference to the riders.

Over the course of my journey I was to learn that many groups up and down the country faced this very same problem.

20

Vyv

After leaving Maggie and Ian we spent almost two whole days following a long, flat, relatively straight main road that went on and on and on, mile after tedious mile, across landscape that changed gradually from open and exposed mountains to thickly forested hills.

Even Taliesin, who as usual was lost in his own little world, had eventually registered that things were getting boring and had started trying to deviate from the route at every available opportunity in order to bring some much needed variation into the equation - but to no avail. In fact the only things to break our otherwise monotonous progress were lorries thundering by, or trains flashing past along the railway running beside us. Then Taliesin would wake up just enough to flinch before settling back into his sombre reveries. All this was accompanied by the steady hum of the M74, which also ran alongside us. If Taliesin had had issues with motorways, lorries, or railways before we hit that stretch of road, he certainly didn't by the time we finally, and with great relief, turned off it at Beattock and struck out across the hills again.

Those long, boring days were broken up by stops with two kind sheep farmers. The first let us camp in a field by a river in Crawford, where the people living in the neighbouring houses made us feel very welcome indeed, bringing me fresh water, cups of tea and coffee, apples for Taliesin, treats for Spirit, and even offering me a shower and breakfast in the morning. The second, based near Johnstonebridge, put us up in his barn that hadn't been mucked out since lambing several months before, and evidently a dog or a fox had been using it frequently for a toilet. Even so, I felt blessed to be out of the rain, which had started off as light drizzle in the morning but was now pelting down outside the barn. Blessed, that is, until the wind changed direction in the night, blowing the rain into the barn through a gap just above where I was sleeping and I woke up cursing in a puddle of water. Thankfully, the following night we would be staying with my friend and mentor, Vyv, and I would be able to dry out my sodden things, have a bath, and once again sleep in a bed!

Vyv Wood Gee was an experienced equestrian traveller and member of the Long Riders' Guild. In 2006, she had ridden more than 1,000 miles from John O'Groats to Land's End with her daughter, Elsa, on their sturdy little Fell ponies. More recently, in 2016, she rode 1,500 miles around Britain, visiting the many iconic white horses that had been carved into the landscape across the centuries.

When I had finally taken the decision to head off on this mad adventure, I'd approached Vyv to ask her advice on routes across Scotland. I have to confess that part of me had been hoping she would talk me out of the idea, tell me I wasn't prepared or experienced enough for such a journey, that it was the wrong time of year, that I needed to do more planning, something - anything! - to put me off and give me a good excuse not to go.

She didn't.

Instead, she went over and above the call of duty, and in one phone call reeled off an entire route - telling me where there were good tracks through Highland estates and across the mountains, where those tracks started, where they emerged, where I might encounter locked gates, who to call if that should happen, and even where to look for accommodation. I scrambled to write down all this information as she rattled it off, barely pausing for breath, even though I had absolutely no idea where any of these places actually were! I tried to sound as if I knew what she was talking about, asking what I hoped were intelligent-sounding questions, and interjecting the occasional sage 'hmmm' and 'I see' in the most confident-sounding voice I could muster, while I struggled to quell the surging feelings of panic that I was really experiencing.

Later on, feeling a little calmer, I sat down and plotted those names onto a map. Sure enough, they formed a perfect, seamless route right the way across Scotland, avoiding major roads and cities. She really knew her stuff, Vyv, and over the weeks that followed she sent me more information about the route and more suggestions on where to stay and where to avoid. Not only that, she had also offered us a place to stop on our way up, and on our way down, too.

Back in August on our way up to Durness, Guy and I had arrived quite late at Vyv's rambling old house just outside Lockerbie. It was wonderful, if a little intimidating, to finally meet her.

She was a short, well-built woman, with a broad, open face framed by a greying tangle of curly dark hair. As we chatted over dinner that night, she struck me as being forthright and open, fiercely determined, strong in her principles and with a very low tolerance for anything she perceived to be bullshit. But for all that fierceness and strength of character, she was caring, attuned, and emotional, too. She made no pretences, wore no masks - she was authentic. I had never met anyone quite like her before.

That evening, as she talked of her many adventures over the years, both on horseback and in horse-drawn wagons, her voice filled with nostalgia for the freedom of the open road, I found myself totally in awe of her - her confidence, knowledge, and above all her courage, will, and determination in the face of all the challenges that the road had thrown at her. Had she undertaken those journeys because she possessed these qualities, I wondered, or did she possess these qualities because of those journeys? And then I wondered, with a sinking heart, whether I possessed any of those qualities at all. Did I have even an ounce of her strength, or a fraction of her courage, her determination, or her stamina? Would I be able to cope with the challenges that lay ahead of me? I didn't know yet, but I was about to find out!

Suddenly I felt very under-qualified and under-prepared for the journey upon which I was about to embark.

And now here I was again, almost a month later and nearly half way home. I was no longer terrified of the unknown or full of doubt and anxiety - either about myself, or my journey. I didn't think I was anywhere near as tough as Vyv, but I was certainly stronger, more confident and more determined than I had given myself credit for, and that was a good start.

We spent a day resting there, Taliesin grazing and having regular feeds - even though he looked as if he'd much rather be on the road - and Spirit sleeping, thoroughly enjoying not having to walk anywhere. Vyv and I pored over my maps which were spread across the enormous kitchen table, looking at the onward route, checking and cross-checking it against her own extensive library of maps. There wasn't much of Britain that Vyv had not traversed on horseback over the years. She was a veritable fountain of knowledge and an excellent mentor. It was wonderful to swap stories from the road, discuss equipment, horses, and all other aspects of equestrian travel with someone as passionate about the topic as I was.

Vyv advised me to arrange my stops in advance once I was back in England. She doubted I would have quite so much luck winging it that side of the border, and because she knew her stuff and was far more experienced than I, I listened and spent a large portion of my day off trying to organise accommodation for the next three or four nights. Once again, Vyv provided some invaluable help, recommending places she knew of, or had stayed at herself.

I have to admit I wasn't all that keen on this pre-planning business, because suddenly it meant I had to reach a certain place by a certain time each day. No more going with the flow or having impromptu days off whenever I felt like it! It was a much more restrictive way to travel, but I knew Vyv was right. We were nearing big cities and people would be less open and less trusting if we simply turned up unannounced, looking for somewhere to camp. Yet for all the sudden restrictiveness, there was actually something reassuring about no longer having to worry about where we would stay each night.

'Wish it were me!' Vyv called out, as she waved us off from the top of her long and winding drive. And I knew that she meant it.

Part 2: England

The route across England

21

England

Equestrians are an odd bunch of people who generally fall into two categories. First, there are the welly-wearers who sport a healthy smattering of hay and dirt, and who spend more time pushing barrows and getting covered in muck than they do actually riding their beloved horses; and then there are the ones who wear pristine white jodhpurs with shiny black, knee length boots, have never mucked out a horse in their entire life, and who can usually be found prancing about in sand schools on big expensive warmbloods, looking down their noses at everyone.

OK, maybe that's a little bit of a generalisation, but it's not all that far off the mark. As equestrian types go I much prefer the former, but the equestrian centre on the outskirts of Carlisle where I was staying that night was teeming with the latter - all of whom looked me up and down with unmasked contempt at my dirty, travel-worn trackies, muddy walking boots, and big shaggy lump of a draught horse loaded up with packs full of camping gear. For all my cheery greetings, not a single one deigned to speak to me.

One of the yard girls showed Taliesin to a stable and looked genuinely shocked when I asked her where I could pitch my tent. Apparently, when I had rung up the day before to book overnight accommodation and had said I was travelling with my horse to Cornwall, they had assumed I meant I was transporting him in a lorry.

However, after first obtaining permission from the sour-faced yard owner - who had absolutely no people skills, but whose love for her animals more than made up for the warmth of character she was lacking - I settled down for the night in an empty stable.

I checked often on Taliesin throughout the evening. He was dripping with sweat at being shut in again, and was making short work of his haylage. At eight o'clock, before I went to sleep, I had to refill his almost empty hay net. Once again, I noticed that all the other horses on the yard had finished their rations, too, and wouldn't get another scrap until eight o'clock the following morning.

When we left, people were beginning to arrive on the yard and horse lorries were rolling up the drive ready for a day of competing. Lots of people stared at us with open curiosity as I got Taliesin ready, carefully weighing and balancing the packs before loading them up onto the saddle, strapping them down firmly with bungee cords and adding a finishing touch of pink hi-viz pack covers and yellow-green leg bands that made us stand out like a fly on a wedding cake. Yet for all their curiosity, not a soul asked me what I was doing or where I was going, but they did ask each other as I slipped out of the gates and up the long drive. And because nobody had spoken to me, not one of them knew the answers!

We had crossed the border into England at Gretna Green the day before, dodging the many wedding parties and ribbon-bedecked limousines as we slipped quietly through the famous little town. Every other building there seemed to be a church, registry office, or wedding reception venue. It was a Saturday morning and the place was heaving. After crossing the River Sark on the outskirts of town we suddenly found ourselves back in England.

It is amazing what a difference a border can make!

On the surface, there was nothing obvious. There were no fences, no checkpoints and no change in language or currency, but all the same, there were noticeable differences. For one, the people were different, and it wasn't just because the accent had changed. The Scots on the whole had been a friendly, open, and interested lot, curious about where we were going and what we were doing. These people south of the border, however, seemed hard, cold, and unfriendly. No-one stopped for a chat, and if I tried to talk to anyone, they looked positively affronted. They were a dour lot indeed! Shops and post offices which had been abundant in nearly every village through which we had passed in Scotland, had vanished this side of the border and those that were still in existence had such limited opening hours that they could not be relied upon for restocking supplies or posting my used maps back home to Cornwall. The roads were busier here, the countryside more crowded, and I had the overwhelming feeling that I was heading in the wrong direction. I should be travelling away from the masses, the mad hustle and bustle of civilisation and heading out into the space, the silence, and the wilderness of the Highlands! It felt wrong, and it felt claustrophobic. Speaking of claustrophobia, the biggest difference of all was that although the landscape looked the same on both sides of the invisible line that divided Scotland from England, our access to it most certainly was not.

In 2003 the Land Reform Act was passed in Scotland, giving people the right to access all land for recreational or educational purposes on the provision they did so responsibly, without causing damage to crops or livestock, and without invading anyone's privacy, i.e. tramping across people's front gardens and the like. This meant that, within reason, my animals and I had been allowed to go pretty much anywhere we pleased in Scotland. Although we had stuck mostly to well-defined tracks and quiet roads, the knowledge that we had every right to be there, and every right to go 'off-piste' should we need to, had been quietly reassuring.

In England, however, this was not the case. Suddenly we found ourselves restricted to roads, and a small handful of designated bridleways - which in my experience were usually few and far between, rarely where you wanted them to be, and often didn't lead anywhere useful at all. If they did, they were so overgrown and poorly signposted that you had to apply a great deal of guesswork to know whether you were headed in the right direction, riding with bated breath and waiting for an irate land owner to pop up from out of nowhere to yell at you for trespassing.

All in all, bridleways are a risky business and can be pretty off-putting, and sure enough, it wasn't long before we came unstuck. Actually, we came a-cropper at the first bridleway we came to.

When we left our stop at the livery yard, I had planned on using a bridleway to avoid several miles of tarmac and a long stretch on a busy A-road. The start of what I took to be the bridleway, which was also the drive up to an old castle, was right on the edge of my map and so the markings were somewhat unclear. However, there was definitely a right of way there, and on the far side of the castle there was unmistakably a bridleway; so I put two and two together and assumed that the bridleway went right the way across, linking up two small lanes. Why on earth wouldn't it? It was no enormous or unwarranted leap of the imagination to make such a reasonable assumption.

It had been the perfect plan!

That is, until we arrived at the bottom of the castle drive where the entrance to the bridleway ought to have been and came face to face with a sign clearly stating 'No Horses'.

How could this not be a bridleway? There was definitely one at the other end of the drive. My map said so. According to the same map, no other bridleways emerged further down this stretch of road, so - by default - this had to be it.

Yet the sign was clear: 'No Horses'.

Feeling somewhat at a loss, I stopped to consider my options.

We had twenty-three miles to cover that day, so detouring and adding yet more miles was not something I wanted to do and I certainly didn't want to have to travel along busy main roads if it could be helped. It was too dangerous. But trespassing wasn't much of an option either, and with a sign quite clearly prohibiting access for horses I couldn't exactly feign ignorance if I got caught.

I was still pondering what to do when a friendly Scottish woman, outside whose house we had stopped, came over to chat. She offered me a coffee and gave Taliesin some apples. The refreshments were gratefully received all round and even Spirit, not wanting to be left out, made a point of chewing up some apples - although they clearly weren't much to her liking because she spat them straight back out again!

I asked the woman about the bridleway and she said we could definitely get on to it if we went up the drive to the castle. She also said that the owner of the castle was not at home that weekend, and nor was his wife, so we should probably just chance it.

Now, I'm not a fan of sneaking across people's property, especially not with a big, slow horse covered in startlingly bright, multi-coloured high-viz gear. It's not exactly subtle! But once in a while needs must and you just have to throw caution and better judgement to the wind and risk it. So, feeling emboldened by that kind woman's reassurance and a good kick of caffeine, we crept up the tree-lined drive towards the old, half-ruined red brick castle, turned off into the farmyard just before the moat, made our way through a couple of gates, and emerged at last onto the bridleway. I breathed a sigh of relief, because here at least, there was no chance of an encounter with an irate landowner.

By the time we'd seen off the herd of curious bullocks, wrestled with numerous gates, battled our way across a mire of thick, black mud, and had finally made it to the road on the other side, we'd barely covered half a mile in what had taken us the best part of an hour. I was now in a foul mood, my feet were wet and muddy, and I decided that I really wasn't a fan of bridleways at all!

22

The North Pennines

After that first debacle, bridleways were used sparingly and with great trepidation. Taliesin seemed to find it easier on roads anyway, because the flat surface meant he didn't have to concentrate quite so hard on what his feet were doing and he tripped over them less. As a result, he walked faster. Spirit was content with tarmac, too, because there weren't all those nasty, dangerous gates to manoeuvre. From that moment forward, we did our utmost to avoid all but the most necessary of off-road routes.

Since crossing back into England, an eerie haze had settled heavy and oppressive over the landscape like a thick, warm blanket, all but obscuring our surroundings. I could just make out the mountains of the Lake District away to the south-west - dark and featureless shapes in the strange atmosphere.

Our route zig-zagged its way through Cumbria, south-east first across the flat Eden Valley that gradually became more undulating as sheep-grazed pastures gave way to the wild and wind-swept slopes of the North Pennines. Shrouded in that strange, thick haze, those rugged hills were little more than vague shapes on the horizon. There, nestled into the steep hillsides at the foot of the Pennines, was Scalehouse Farm B&B, with a cosy little camping barn attached. After a shower and good meal, I bedded down for the night, and drifted off to sleep listening to the rain falling softly on the skylight.

From there we went westward again towards Penrith, where we stopped at Happy Hooves riding centre, which also ran an RDA group. Spirit and I slept in a horse lorry that night, sheltering from the torrential rain that had begun to fall just after we'd arrived, while Taliesin roamed contentedly about their pastures, sampling the lush grass and oblivious to the weather.

In the morning we headed east towards the Pennines once more, making our way along narrow lanes that dipped and climbed the shallow hills, and wound through sleepy little villages where nothing seemed to stir.

Many of the towns and villages in that area bore the suffix 'by' (Appleby, Sourby, Soulby), meaning 'settlement' or 'village' in Old Norse. It was fascinating to think that, to this day, those names carried in them the memory of Viking invaders who had settled these lands more than a thousand years before.

As we neared the Pennines again, the countryside became less inhabited, bleaker, and more open, rising steadily towards the towering escarpment of those wild hills. Here we saw fewer people, fewer cars, and the land was silent but for the bleating of sheep and the singing of birds. Eventually, leaving the road behind, we braved another bridleway which brought us right up to the door of a spooky old camping barn standing alone in the middle of a field. We spent the night there and I delighted in making tea with the wild spearmint I'd found growing in a hedgerow earlier in the day. Then I nearly made myself sick in a reckless attempt to preserve my own limited food supplies, by eating some old pasta that had been left in the damp cupboards of the barn by previous visitors from who knows how long ago.

The barn was cold, dark, and damp, and it creaked horribly throughout the night. Although I slept in a bed and had the use of a kettle, a kitchen, and a toilet - luxuries of the highest order - I was glad to leave it again in the morning because I'm sure the place was haunted and it really gave me the creeps.

Still the haze persisted and I had only a vague, distorted impression of the huge hills around me but every now and then, the sun would break through the heavy veil, suddenly illuminating the sweeping slopes of the distant hillsides and setting the thick white atmosphere aglow with a seemingly sourceless light.

For five days I wandered in that strange, silent haze, seeing nothing of the North Pennines. I felt that the countryside must have been magnificent there, but I couldn't know for sure!

My mood was starting to change. Like the haze, it was becoming heavy and oppressive.

Perhaps because since leaving the Highlands, it had started to feel as though the world were closing in on me, becoming more crowded with every mile, and at the same time colder and less welcoming. Or maybe it was because, since leaving Vyv's, I'd had very little meaningful interaction with people. With all these prearranged stops I had been largely left to my own devices, and as a result had not been experiencing the same spontaneous warmth, kindness, and hospitality of strangers that had brought me so much joy and reassurance in the better side of human nature.

I have never considered myself to be a particularly sociable person, and have always been content in my own company for long periods of time; but this journey was teaching me the value of human interaction and the positive effect that it had - lifting my mood, boosting my morale, and pulling me out of my own repetitive thought cycles.

Whatever the reason, one thing was certain - in all that haze without the beauty of my surroundings to distract me, my focus had begun to turn inwards and with each passing day I sank ever deeper into myself, my thoughts, and the all-enveloping silence.

There's that old cliché about people 'finding' themselves on long and difficult journeys, and there's a truth in that. When you travel alone, after a time you are inevitably and inescapably confronted with yourself in the harsh light of reality. Hours, days, and weeks spent alone with yourself in silence, far away from the many easy distractions of the modern world, force you to take a long, soul-searching look at yourself - your strengths, weaknesses, faults and failings. It is difficult, sometimes brutal work, but an integral part of the journey and out there on the bleak, windswept hills of the Pennines, that process of getting to know myself began in earnest.

At the Fat Lamb Inn near Ravenstonedale we picked up the Pennine Bridleway. It was well signposted, the surface was good, and even the gates were just about manoeuvrable without dismounting! Taliesin still couldn't quite get the hang of opening and closing the gates, however, and tried to barge through most of them, while Spirit still got in a tizz and shot through them as soon as they were open a crack, almost pulling me out of the saddle and choking herself in the process. But somehow we managed, and apart from that, the going was surprisingly good.

We followed that bridleway up to the top of a high ridge between Little Fell and Wild Boar Fell, where a sudden strong wind whipped at us savagely, tearing at my hair and clothing and pulling on my map case, which flapped wildly about my neck. In spite of all that flapping, Taliesin didn't bat an eyelid. He's a good sensible horse and clearly has better things to think about.

I was glad to descend on the other side of the ridge, scrambling down the steep, muddy hillside. When we reached the road below, I decided to stick to it as it was sheltered, quiet, and the going was much nicer for both of my animals. It was better than climbing up and down steep inclines on stony tracks, with a cold wind blowing and no view to look at. Anyway, why ride three sides of a square in triple the amount of time when you can ride a straight line in a quarter? Such was my mood that day!

We trudged wearily on along a dull road for miles, all sunk deep in our own thoughts. Then we climbed and climbed up over an enormous lump of a hill, down a steep descent, and finally ended up in the village of Cowgill. There we managed to find a field to camp in for the night, because for all my trying, I'd had no luck finding anywhere to stop in advance.

To my delight, the field was not far from the village pub. After getting my tent set up in the heavy rain that had suddenly started to fall, I made my way down, armed with my journal and all geared up for a cosy night drying out in front of a roaring fire with some human company. It would be blissful and just what I needed to lift my rather low spirits.

Except that when we got there, the owner of the pub told me flatly that they didn't allow dogs inside under any circumstances!

My low spirits plummeted still further. It would be unfair to leave Spirit tied up outside in the pouring rain while I sat inside in the warm and dry, eating nice food and enjoying myself. So we turned around and made our wet and utterly deflated way back to the tent to eat yet another boring meal of plain, boiled pasta, all the while cursing the only country pub I had ever come across that did not allow dogs.

Suddenly, I felt very lonely and very miserable.

23

Conversations

On the sixth day the haze finally dispersed, and at last we were able to take in the scenery.

Sweeping moorland stretched away on all sides. Hills brown with dead rushes, bracken, and wind-burnt grasses rose up to high ridges, and fell steeply away into deep, sparsely wooded river valleys where the leaves on the trees were only just beginning to fade.

Ahead of us rose a cluster of small fells, around whose rugged crowns clouds scudded before the strong wind that was blowing. As we made our way along Ribblesdale, the wind dropped, the day warmed, and my mood lifted.

The barren hillsides, which were interspersed with towering outcrops of grooved and weathered limestone, gave way to rolling green pastures full of sheep and dairy cows, all enclosed by neat, grey, dry-stone walls. Cotton-wool clouds drifted idly across blue skies, unhurried now by the wind, casting shadows here and there on the rolling green hillsides. It was like a picture from a storybook. The English countryside at its finest!

To make up for what I'd missed the night before, we stopped for lunch at a pub in Horton in Ribblesdale where I sat out in the warm sunshine eating chips and onion rings while Taliesin and Spirit snoozed beside me.

Two young men who were walking north along the Pennine Way stopped at the pub for a beer. One came over to chat and we had the same conversation I'd had with nearly everyone that we'd met on our travels, every single day, sometimes several times a day, for the whole of the last month. It was the Where-Are-You-Going-What-Are-You-Doing conversation, and while I usually tried to sound enthusiastic whenever I had this conversation, I had just had it with the landlady of the pub when I'd ordered my food, then again with two tourists coming into the pub as I was on my way back out, then with a young family outside the pub, and then yet again with the chef who had brought me out my lunch. By the time this young man came over to have it, I was in no mood for the long version of the conversation, and opted instead to have the shorter, more to the point version, that went something like this:

Man: 'You look like you've come far.' A classic opener.

Me: 'Yep.'

Man: 'Where are you headed?'

Me: 'Cornwall.'

Man: 'What?'

Me: 'Cornwall.' I said it a little louder.

Man: 'Oh wow! That's a long way! Where did you start?'

Me: 'Top of Scotland.'

Man: 'What?'

Me: 'Top of Scotland.' This was getting a little repetitive and my chips were going cold.

Man, oblivious to chip situation: 'That's mad! How long has it taken you?'

Me: 'About a month.'

Man: 'When will you get to Cornwall?'

Me: 'Before winter comes.'

Man: 'And you're staying in B&Bs?'

Me: 'No.'

Man: 'What?'

Me: 'No. I'm camping.' Sort of.

Man: 'You're crazy!'

This was the usual conclusion that people drew, long or short version of this conversation.

Me: 'Yep.'

'Oi!' the man shouted to his friend. 'Come and hear what this crazy girl's doing!'

And so the conversation happened all over again with the second man, pretty much verbatim, and I resigned myself to having cold chips.

'It's a pity we're heading in the opposite direction to you,' they said before they left. 'We could have looked after you for the night.'

I wasn't quite sure how to take that remark, but somehow I was glad we were going in opposite directions!

Another conversation I frequently had was the Finding-A-Place-To-Stop conversation. I'd got this one down to a fine art by now, and it went something along these lines:

Me: 'Excuse me! Hi. I'm sorry to bother you, but I was wondering if you could help me. I'm riding my horse from Scotland to Cornwall and we're looking for somewhere to camp for the night. I don't suppose you'd know of anyone around here who might be able to help? All we need is a field for the horse and somewhere to pitch my tent.'

Even if we were talking to someone who was quite clearly a farmer, standing in an obviously empty field of good grass, the trick was to keep the question broad, rather than direct, giving them as many easy ways out as possible, and never trying to force them into letting us camp on their land. It's no good being pushy, or entitled; that doesn't get you anywhere.

What usually happened then, in the Finding-A-Place-To-Stop conversation, was that the person I was asking would look a little taken aback, scratch their head, say no they couldn't think of anyone, and then they'd start the Where-Are-You-Going-What-Are-You-Doing conversation, which I would have in full, with as much patience as I could muster. By the end of that conversation, whoever I was talking to would have had time to suss me out and decide I wasn't about to murder them in their beds or rob them blind. In most cases they would then go on to offer us a field, or if they didn't have one, would point us in the direction of someone who did.

By the time we reached Giggleswick I was starting to think it was time to stop. Again, I hadn't managed to arrange anything for the night and had left it up to Providence to provide. Sure enough, between Rathmell and Wigglesworth, we encountered a dairy farmer who at first had 'ummed' and 'ahhed' and scratched his head doubtfully when I asked him about somewhere to camp, but once we'd finished the Where-Are-You-Going-What-Are-You-Doing conversation and he'd decided I wasn't a psycho axe murderer, he offered us the corner of a field for the night.

24

The Spider

There was a spider on the ceiling. I don't like spiders. They scare me, what with their fat bodies and unnecessary number of legs. This spider was sitting right above the bed and the ceiling was so high I hadn't a hope of swatting it off to a less offensive position, which made me decidedly uncomfortable.

'Don't be so silly!' I told myself firmly. 'Spiders sit about on ceilings all the time. What are the chances it's going to fall on you?'

But all the same, as I wrote up the day's events in my journal I kept glancing furtively upwards to make sure the spider hadn't moved.

The day had started badly, when - just after I had finished packing away my tent - the heavens opened and a cold rain bucketed down onto our little party. Within seconds we were all soaked through. The rain had been accompanied by an icy wind that sent a chill through my sodden clothing, freezing me to the bone and numbing my fingers. My toes, too, were frozen where they sat in the puddles of near-glacial water that had formed in my boots. I was miserable.

To make matters worse, I had just discovered that Taliesin had a sore on his left side in front of the girth where it had suddenly, and inexplicably, begun to rub.

But I was comforted by the thought that a bed and a hot bath awaited me at the end of the day, and that we were to have a few days off to rest and relax. Things would look better with a bit of warm hospitality and a good night's sleep.

My host for the night, Cosima Towneley, who was the Conservative County Councillor for Burnley, had rung me a few days earlier to offer us a stop over on our way through, and I had gratefully accepted.

I rang her when we were a few miles away from our destination and a short while later a turquoise Nissan Micra came roaring up the road, squealed to a halt opposite a pub, and out leapt a stout woman in her early fifties. She had a ruddy complexion, an unruly crop of short grey hair, and was wearing a checked shirt, buttoned up to the chin, with a dark green waistcoat over the top. She looked to me like the sort of person who enjoyed shooting things and was partial to galloping about the countryside with a pack of hounds in hot pursuit of a fox, shouting 'Tally-ho!' and swigging liberally from a hip flask. My heart sank.

'Cathleen! Hullo!' she boomed at us, her deep, posh voice unapologetically loud, and filled with all the self-assuredness and sense of entitlement that is the birth right of the upper classes.

'Oh God!' I thought, with sinking heart 'What have I let myself in for?'

I could tell she was thinking the same as she looked us up and down, taking in my dishevelled, mud splattered appearance, and strange collection of animals. One eyebrow raised slightly in surprise. Clearly we were not quite what she had been expecting.

After the initial shock had passed, Cosima gained mastery of herself once more and, beaming determinedly, took firm command of the situation, gave me directions for the final leg of the route, and met us at every junction to ensure we did not become lost.

In this manner, at long last, we arrived in her stable yard at the top of a long, pot-holed drive.

No sooner had I tied up my animals and begun untacking Taliesin, then Spirit took it upon herself to pounce on Bat, Cosima's boisterous young Whippet, who was pestering her unsuccessfully for a game. Waiting until he came within reach of her lead, Spirit suddenly lunged, grabbed him by the throat and pinned him to the ground, snarling ferociously, while Bat's loud yelps of surprise filled the air. Getting hold of Spirit, I managed to prise open her jaws and the terrified Bat flew off down the drive with his tail between his legs and Cosima marching along in his wake yelling 'Bat! Batty! Bat!' at the top of her lungs.

I was mortified.

'I'll not have it!' Cosima declared angrily when she returned a few minutes later, red-faced, panting, and without Bat. 'No. It simply won't do. It'll be far too upsetting for Papa. I can't have her in the house!'

I couldn't argue. Spirit had behaved atrociously!

The defiant-looking Spirit was locked up in a stable to reflect on her uncivilised behaviour and Taliesin was turned out into an enormous field with rich pickings of grass, some nice hay, and a good feed. I piled into the tiny car with all my belongings and we drove off down to the house where we found the rather shaken, but thankfully unscathed, Bat waiting for us. Although Cosima softened a little, I knew we were off to a very bad start.

The house was a large, gloomy, and rather imposing affair, built in mottled sandstone and set into the side of the sweeping Lancashire moors. Inside, it was like stepping back in time. The hallways were panelled in dark wood and hung with portraits of various ancestors, old maps, and other documents of historical interest pertaining to the Towneley family.

Cosima lived there with her ninety-six-year-old father, Sir Simon Towneley - formerly High Sheriff and Lord Lieutenant of Lancashire, an accomplished cellist and authority on seventeenth century Venetian opera. Her mother, the late Lady Mary Towneley, had been a keen horsewoman - completing several long distance rides in her day - and a strong advocate for equestrian rights of way. She had also founded the local RDA group.

We entered through the back door of the house and Cosima led the way up the servant's stairs to the nursery wing. I was to sleep in the old nanny's room. It had a lofty ceiling, faded wallpaper on walls that bore a collection of framed paintings and sketches, and on the floor was a green felt carpet that looked as though it had seen better days.

Scattered about the room were pieces of mismatched old furniture, all covered in a fine layer of dust.

The bathroom was next door to my bedroom, and gaudy riverside scenes had been painted on each wall from floor to ceiling. Whenever the ancient pull-chain toilet flushed there was a deafening noise and the whole floor shook. Cosima said she thought the wing had last been refurbished in Victorian times. It certainly looked like it.

After a short soak in a hot bath, I went down to find my hosts. I was dressed in some of Cosima's clothing, because my only clean change of clothes, namely a t-shirt and a pair of comfortable pyjama bottoms, were deemed too inappropriate for dinner attire ('Papa would not approve!'). She had fished out a checked shirt and a rather hideous pair of three-quarter length brown trousers that were several sizes too big. With no belt in sight, and worried they might fall down, I'd had to scrunch up the waistband at one side and fasten it with a hairband. Needless to say, I looked very comical and not a little ridiculous as I made my way down to dinner.

Champagne was served in the library, my journey toasted, then Sir Simon instructed me to sit in the armchair opposite him, next to the open fire, which sent long shadows flickering over the shelves full of old books that lined the walls from floor to ceiling on every side.

Although frail of body, Sir Simon's mind was as sharp as a whip and he immediately set about questioning me, his thin voice cold and severe. Who were my parents? What did they do? Where had I been raised? Where had I been educated? What did I do for a living? I sat squirming under his stern, unwavering gaze as he peered at me over the tops of his spectacles. It felt as though I were sitting some kind of exam to win his approval - and I was failing miserably. The whole thing was making me feel rather uncomfortable.

'Don't you think it terribly ill-mannered to inflict your dietary requirements on the people who offer you hospitality on your journey?' Sir Simon asked suddenly, when, after trying a few different topics of conversation, we had failed to find any solid common ground for a lengthy discussion. He was, of course, referring to my being a vegan. 'I was always taught that one should eat what one is given.' he continued, rather pointedly. 'Being a vegetarian for moral reasons, that I can understand, but to not eat eggs or dairy? I think you're taking it too far!'

I was slightly taken aback at this somewhat dismissive view of my dietary ethics. But, I reminded myself, at almost a hundred years of age, my host was a product of his era, his class, and his upbringing. I highly doubted that all the arguments in favour of a vegan diet - the appalling animal welfare standards, dairy and egg-production's links to the meat industry, the over-use of antibiotics within animal agriculture which is contributing to a world-wide antibiotic resistance crisis, the environmental destruction and climate issues caused by the mass production of animals to feed an over-populated planet, or even the health benefits of a plant-based diet - to name but a few, would have any influence on his strong and rather archaic opinions. Nevertheless, I presented a small handful of points for discussion.

Sir Simon would have none of it, however, and told me flatly that he thought I was wrong on all counts, that my morals were flawed, and implied that - because it was such an inconvenience to my hosts - I really ought to stop being so childishly impolite and eat whatever was on offer.

Things had got off to a bad start with Cosima, and they certainly weren't looking up yet. If anything they were getting worse.

'Well, I did forewarn Cosima - ' I said feebly.

'The day before you arrived!' she interjected incredulously from where she was perched on a stool, puffing away at a cigarette.

'- and I did say that if it were an inconvenience, then I was more than happy to cater for myself.' I finished, withering quietly and wishing I could be up in the stable with Spirit where at least I would have been able to relax.

'Well I think that's extremely rude!' Sir Simon exclaimed, outraged. 'You can't just go rummaging around in somebody else's kitchen! That's very ill-mannered! Don't you agree, Cosi?'

She did.

I was genuinely shocked. I had never come across anyone who would object to such a thing, or take offence at it.

I realised suddenly that here were two very different and opposing worlds colliding under one roof. Theirs was a world built on a series of bizarre social constructs such as class and breeding, etiquette and propriety, and mine is a world where the only thing that really matters is whether or not someone is a decent human being. I didn't understand their world or any of the rules that went with it, and they didn't understand mine; so, feeling decidedly uncomfortable and more than a little out of place, I changed the subject, and shortly afterwards we went through to the dining room for dinner.

I had been relieved to get away from my forbidding hosts and escape to the sanctuary of my room that night. Cosima had softened enough to allow Spirit to come and sleep in the room with me, for which I was deeply grateful, but now there was the question of that infernal spider, sitting just out of reach, right above my bed.

I couldn't relax with it there, but there was no way I could ask Cosima for a hoover, or a long implement to remove it. I had already inadvertently offended her and her father with my vegan diet and willingness to rummage about in their kitchen. If they felt so strongly about such trifles then they would most certainly find this insulting. And although the spider scared me, it didn't scare me nearly as much as my hosts!

I had almost managed to convince myself that spiders don't go round falling off of ceilings, and was just about to call it a night, when, looking up once more, my heart stopped.

The spider was gone.

I stifled an involuntary shriek and shook my head furiously, brushing wildly at my hair, and barely managed to stop myself screaming blue murder as the fat black body with its too many spindly legs flopped down onto the bed covers in front of me. Without thinking I swiped at it, knocking it down between the bed and the wall where I couldn't get to it, but I knew it was still very much alive.

Oh God! I shuddered all over, my skin crawling as I leapt out of bed and landed next to the rather startled looking Spirit.

I couldn't sleep there. Not with that creature still alive and lurking about under the bed. What if it crawled into the bed in the night? Or fell on me again? I couldn't do it! That spider definitely had it in for me.

So I did the only thing I could do under the circumstances and, getting hold of the bed, I pulled it away from the wall. There was the sickening sound of tearing material. I looked down in dismay at the large rend in the old moth eaten carpet where the leg of the bed had torn right through to the wooden floorboards beneath.

Fuck! Shit! Fuckity fuck fuck fuck! This whole situation was going from bad to worse! Why had I moved the bed? Oh God! This was turning into a nightmare. These people clearly didn't like me, we had nothing in common, I was stuck here for a few days because Taliesin needed time to heal, and no matter what I said or did, nothing seemed to be going right. To top it all off, I had just torn the sodding carpet trying to escape a pathetic little spider!

But the damage was done. There was nothing for it but to try and cover the tear up in the morning when I moved the bed back, but for now it was staying where it was in the middle of the room, well away from the spider.

Peering cautiously down the far side of the bed, I could see no sign of the offending creature amongst the thick layers of dust, but I knew it was there somewhere.

25

Dinner with the Towneleys

In the morning, I carefully pushed the bed back into position against the wall and, to my relief, the tear in the carpet was hidden. Phew!

But there was still no sign of the spider.

I made my way down to breakfast, steeling myself for yet more awkwardness. Sir Simon was alone in the dining room, finishing off a cup of tea and leafing through the selection of newspapers that lay scattered across the table.

After a few strained attempts at polite chit-chat, I reached gratefully for a magazine and buried myself in some thoroughly uninteresting articles.

Cosima was out for the day so I wandered up to see Taliesin, who was grazing contentedly in his enormous field, stopping every now and then to gaze into the middle distance, or to groom with one of the livery horses across the wall. The girth gall was looking marginally better, but he flinched when I applied some antiseptic cream. Taliesin is pretty stoic and rarely lets on if something's hurting, so I knew the sore must have been bothering him. I doubted he'd be ready to hit the road again the following day.

That evening, Cosima was dining with friends so she left me in charge of serving Sir Simon his dinner. I was mildly amused that in Cosima's absence it became suddenly acceptable for me to become fully acquainted with the intimate workings of the kitchen, which only the night before had been so strictly off limits. But I bit my tongue, said nothing, and tried to be a polite guest. After all, these people had been kind enough to offer me hospitality.

Dinner was a truly painful affair with many halting attempts at short-lived conversations, and plenty of long, awkward silences.

Sir Simon and I retraced much of the ground we had covered the evening before, searching desperately for something comfortable to talk about: where had I been raised? Where had I been educated? Who were my parents? And still the answers were unsatisfactory.

My father was Irish, born and raised in Dublin, my mother American. No class or breeding here, I'm afraid! I had attended a Steiner school, which although a private school, was probably too liberal and alternative for Sir Simon's tastes. What about my religious orientation? Had I been raised a Catholic? He tried hopefully, because the Towneleys were an old recusant family and still practiced their faith devoutly. But sadly that one fell short, too, because although my father had been raised a Catholic, he had renounced it soon after leaving Dublin; and my grandfather, who had been a follower of the faith, was a staunch republican, and had been heavily involved in the IRA. Once again, conversation petered out and silence endured.

I don't know whether it was a last desperate resort on his part to break the tense silence, but suddenly, and quite out of nowhere, Sir Simon asked from across his plate of shrivelled partridge:

'How did you vote?'

'Excuse me?' I was wrestling with a floret of slightly under-cooked broccoli and the question caught me completely off guard.

'Did you vote to remain or leave?' He was referring to the referendum that had taken place the year before in 2016, to determine whether or not the United Kingdom should remain within the European Union. It was a rather controversial topic, and one about which most people felt quite strongly. Surely he shouldn't be asking me this sort of thing over dinner? 'Oh god! Here we go!' I thought, bracing myself.

'I voted to remain,' I said, hesitantly, knowing that whatever I said it was bound to be the wrong thing.

'So did I.'

This genuinely surprised me. Here at last was the common ground we'd so desperately been seeking! Perhaps this shared political view would be enough to transcend some of the prevailing awkwardness and bring us together. I was all for it! Maybe I had been too quick to judge. Perhaps he wasn't so bad after all.

'But I've since changed my mind.'

Ah. Perhaps not then.

'Oh? How come?' I was genuinely intrigued.

'Because the European government is so corrupt and undemocratic,' he said, matter-of-factly.

'But so is ours!' I blurted out before I could stop myself.

I knew I shouldn't have said it. I knew I should have kept my mouth shut, been neutral and meekly gone along with whatever he said. But it was too late.

'Well I don't think you can say that!' he spluttered, his voice rising in sudden rage and his face turning a deep shade of crimson. 'You need to substantiate that remark!' Before I had a chance, he continued: 'In fact, Britain has one of the best, most democratic governments in the world! And actually I think you're very ill-educated and need to grow up!'

I shrank under this volley of criticism and unmasked contempt. Sir Simon absolutely terrified me, if I was perfectly honest, but I tried not to let it show. And while I disagreed wholeheartedly with everything he had just said, somehow I couldn't see us having a nice, civilised discussion about an out-dated, first-past-the-post electoral system; corrupt, tax dodging politicians; MPs' expenses scandals and their unprecedented pay-rises; or the Conservative government's brutal cuts to public services in the name of Austerity. And that was just the tip of the iceberg! It was almost on a par with the corruption inside the Catholic Church - another topic, I felt, that was best left well enough alone.

So I bit my tongue, and shoved a forkful of broccoli into my mouth to keep it otherwise engaged lest I let something else slip that might make the evening any worse.

When at last, and with great relief, I got back up to my room, I found the spider sitting in its original position over the bed again. Even though I didn't want to hurt it, and I felt very guilty indeed, I was also in no mood for a repeat of the night before, so, taking advantage of Cosima's absence and Sir Simon's hardness of hearing, I fetched a hoover that I'd passed in the hallway at the top of the stairs, and I dealt with the spider once and for all.

The following evening, with Sir Simon in bed suffering from a cold, Cosima and I sat in the kitchen having dinner. I felt a little more relaxed in Sir Simon's absence.

Cosima had given me free range of the kitchen, letting me cook my own dinner, while she had seen to hers. She was now working her way steadily through a bottle of wine, while I worked my way through a nice pot of tea.

While we dined, Cosima quizzed me on my views, asking me my stance on all kinds of things such as fox hunting, the EU referendum, immigration, the legalisation of cannabis, and gay marriage. She seemed genuinely curious and open to hearing my perspective, but suffice it to say we agreed on very little.

However, although strong in her opinions, Cosima was a great deal more diplomatic than her austere father, and she listened carefully to my views before presenting her arguments to the contrary. The discussion that evening was much more two-sided than it had been the night before.

I could see why she, as a Conservative, had won an election in what was a predominantly Labour area. She was passionate and driven, a tireless campaigner for the things she believed in, and she had an unfailing energy and enthusiasm, accompanied by a remarkable ability to get things done. If you needed action, Cosima was unquestionably your woman. I doubted anything could stand in her way once she set her mind on a target. She was a formidable force! And because I admired those qualities, even though I wasn't too sure about either her views, or her political persuasion, I warmed to her.

I was just about to call it a night and head up to bed when Cosima suddenly said:

'Do you know, Cathleen, you're quite well grounded for a hippy! When I saw you on the day you arrived, looking all scruffy, with a ring in your nose, riding a shaggy pony with a dog on a bit of string, I thought to myself "Oh fuck!" but actually you're a really interesting person! And I know Papa's given you a hard time, but he has really enjoyed having you here.'

Crikey! I had made it. I had passed the test. Somehow, in spite of all my numerous social faux pas, I had actually managed to gain just the tiniest bit of their respect and approval!

Likewise, for all our opposing views and the very little common ground between us, I couldn't help but admire Cosima. In her own right she was a strong, fiery woman, with an incredible amount of motivation and determination. She was thick-skinned, hard-headed, didn't care what anyone thought about her, and she stuck firmly by her principles. I like that in a person! And in spite of all the awkwardness and tension of the last few days, I was grateful for the hospitality that Cosima and Sir Simon had offered me, and for the insights they had given me into a world so vastly different than my own.

So on that positive note, the evening ended and I retired to my room ... only to find that Spirit had had diarrhoea all over the torn, mouldy carpet. It was time to get back on the road!

26

Back on the Road

He was gone!

One minute I had been sitting happily astride Taliesin's broad and powerful back, and the next I found myself standing, feet flat on the ground with nothing but empty space where my horse should have been.

Taliesin had vanished from under me, dropping suddenly and without warning into thick mud that came half way up his belly. He looked just as surprised as I was.

When we left that morning, Cosima had given me her map to use. It was an Ordnance Survey Explorer map and, with a scale of 1:25000, it was much more detailed than the 1:50000 scale Landranger maps I had been using throughout the journey.

I was used to my own maps. I understood how to read them, knew how much distance we covered in how much time, and so far, in the five weeks we had been on the road, not once had we become properly lost. But Cosima had insisted I take her map because, she said, it was better than mine, and without it we would definitely lose ourselves in the maze of bridleways, footpaths, and tracks that crossed the moor over to our next stop at Wardle. All attempts at resistance had been futile. When Cosima thought she was right, there was just no arguing with her. So, for an easy life, I had gone along with it. Except it wasn't making life easy, it was making life incredibly difficult, because I really couldn't get my head around reading this new and much more detailed map with its very different scale and strange markings, and I had absolutely no idea where we were.

'The first part is straightforward. Just follow the bridleway up to the top of the hill until you reach the boundary wall, then follow that. You can't go wrong! It's a very substantial wall and it's all marked on the map,' Cosima had assured me, as we set off from the yard that morning.

We had reached a wall - several of them in fact - and there was nothing to say which one was the boundary wall. None stood out from the rest in any particular way; they were just, well, walls! One wall, which was in good repair, veered off to our right, and another wall, that was falling down in several places, carried straight on beyond a gate. I had no idea which one to follow and as usual there were no bridleway signs to help me out.

Surveying my surroundings, I noticed what looked like a very muddy track leading off to our right, loosely following the course of the more solid of the two walls. So, making an educated guess that this must be the substantial boundary wall that Cosima had assured me I could not miss, we set off along the track without further hesitation.

Unfortunately, what had appeared to be a wide, muddy track leading up the hill had not been a track at all and had, in fact, been a bog into whose reeking black depths Taliesin had sunk.

This was not good.

I stepped clear of him as he began to flounder, trying desperately to gain a foothold in the thick, soup-like mire, while I looked on, helpless. You hear of horses dying in bogs, any efforts to free themselves resulting in them becoming further immersed in the mud until, too tired to struggle any more, they drown - a slow and horrible death. Oh God! What should I do? I didn't want to lose my faithful old Taliesin. Not like this!

I felt a surge of panic. This couldn't be happening!

Suddenly, with an almighty heave, Taliesin managed to pull his front legs free of the mud and onto solid ground. Then, with an enormous effort, he dragged the rest of himself out of the bog. I breathed a sigh of relief.

He was plastered from the shoulder down in thick, black, foul-smelling muck, but apart from looking dazed and a little shaken, he seemed to be otherwise unscathed. Luckily he wasn't wearing a saddle or carrying any gear that day either because, in order to give his girth gall another day to heal, Cosima had very kindly offered to drive our things over to our stop that evening. I wondered whether Taliesin would have managed to get himself out of the bog had he been weighed down with the saddle and all our equipment. I shuddered at the thought of what might have happened.

After letting Taliesin graze for a few minutes to regain his composure, I decided to try our luck following the other, tumbled-down wall on the far side of the gate. At least the ground there appeared to be more solid.

That wall, as it turned out, was the right one, and we spent the day wandering without further ado across the wet and windswept moors to Wardle, where we stayed on a dairy farm turned livery yard that was owned by the loveliest old Yorkshireman named John. He was true salt of the earth and a warmer, more genuine old soul you could not wish to meet. He was all heart, had a lovely smile, and through his easy contentment with life, and the joy he seemed to find in the simplest of things, he was a welcome contrast to the previous few days of awkward tension and unwitting breaches of etiquette.

I made camp on the cold concrete floor of his old milking parlour, where I slept well and awoke feeling more positive and well rested than I had in a long time.

27

The Peak District

We were still making our way along sections of the Pennine Bridleway across grey, open moorland. Then, dropping down into pretty dales, we slipped quietly through picturesque villages that had sprung up centuries before around the once thriving textile industries, whose ghosts lay scattered throughout the north of England. On the riverbanks stood the remnants of old mills and factories, huge and imposing, many of which had fallen into ruin or else been converted into houses and apartments in what were now sleepy little villages. It was a far cry from the noisy, bustling places they would have been in the times of the Industrial Revolution.

One night we stayed on the outskirts of Manchester, where Jen, the young woman who ran a stables there, invited me into the house she shared with her partner and her brother, offering me a bed in the spare room. Both men, she said, had been apprehensive about letting me stay - worried that I might rob them, or worse, murder them all in their sleep! It was understandable, I suppose, that here near the bigger cities people would be less trusting and less willing to open their doors to a complete stranger. I was thankful that Jen had enough faith in the better side of human nature to invite me into their home. I was always humbled by that simple, yet courageous act, when people opened their doors to offer me a haven for the night.

That night not only did Jen offer me hospitality and a bed in a warm, cosy house, but she also found me a violin to play. Music was a wonderful distraction that evening. How I had missed playing! I was surprised that my fingers could still find their way around the strings enough to coax out a tune or two.

The following day the character of the landscape began to change as broad, rolling moorland gave way to the higher, more defined hills of the Peak District. Yellow-grey grasses on bare hillsides stood out stark against the vivid green fields of the settled valleys below us, bright against the dark, foreboding October skies which threatened a rain that luckily did not fall. The Pennine Bridleway climbed up steep slopes and down into deep dells, crossing over little stone bridges which spanned tumbling streams along whose sheltered banks birch, ash, rowan and hawthorn trees grew in abundance, clinging tenuously to existence in that harsh and unforgiving landscape. These wild hills gave way to more tame and settled countryside as we left the Pennine Bridleway and its multitude of irritating gates behind us, and plodded gently along quiet lanes past working farms and old stone cottages. Eventually, dropping down into a deep gorge along whose bottom a river carved its way, snaking between the steep, wooded sides of the Derbyshire hills, we picked up the Monsal Trail. That was a nice flat, well-surfaced track, which followed the course of an old railway, running high along the side of the gorge. In places the trail led through long, dimly lit tunnels where the steady clip-clop of Taliesin's hooves reverberated in the pressing darkness, accompanied by the drip-drop of water falling from the rough-hewn rocks of the tunnel roof. But not once did Taliesin hesitate when entering those gaping black entrances, nor did the ringing echoes of his heavy footfalls seem to bother him at all as he strode along with Spirit trotting ever at his side.

I travelled through this beautiful, changing landscape in a daze, sometimes walking, sometimes riding, but barely taking in my surroundings at all. I had slept badly the night before and had woken up feeling under the weather. By the end of the day I had lost my voice, was coughing painfully and my throat felt as though I had been swallowing broken glass. All in all, I felt rotten.

We had been offered hospitality for the night at the home of Janine Frost, secretary of the Helen Atkin RDA group in Buxton, who lived not far from the Monsal Trail. I was looking forward to a hot bath and a good night's sleep to shake off this cold, but when, at the end of the long and winding drive, I saw the many gables and tall chimney stacks of the enormous old manor house peeking out above the treetops, I groaned. Was this going to be a repeat of my rather awkward stay with the Towneleys?

I looked on warily as the big electric gates swung slowly open and the willowy figure of Janine, a tall, blonde woman, clad in long riding boots and dark jodhpurs, came striding out to meet us. As soon as she began to chat in an easy-going, friendly manner, all my worries vanished. She was lovely! And her friendly warmth made me feel instantly at ease. So much so, that when she invited us to rest there for a day while I fought off my quickly progressing cold, I accepted her offer gratefully, and without hesitation.

28

Decisions

I spent my day off with Janine at the riding school in Buxton where the Helen Atkin RDA group ran their sessions. There I had the pleasure of meeting the enthusiastic and dedicated team of volunteers, and the equally enthusiastic and motivated team of riders, some of whom had even competed at the RDA's Regional and National Championships. They were certainly one of the more proactive, driven RDA groups that I encountered on my journey, and the enthusiasm of both the volunteers and the clients was infectious.

When we left Janine's the next day, I was feeling a whole lot better. My sore throat had gone and my nose was no longer streaming. I had a bit of a cough but that wouldn't take much to clear, and the cherry on the cake was that Taliesin's girth gall, which had caused me so much worry over the past few days, was now healing nicely. It had been a good stay. I was well rested, in high spirits, and ready to face the challenges of the road once more!

Janine rode out with us for the first few miles on one of her leggy hunters, who worked up quite a sweat and marched along at a terrific pace, while Taliesin languidly kept up with no effort at all; his long, ground-covering strides making it feel as though he were plodding along at a snail's pace.

The whole way, Janine chatted happily about this and that and, as we passed one enormous manor house after the other, she filled me in on little bits of local history. Derbyshire, she said, had once been the hub of society when the Duke of Devonshire had lived at Chatsworth House in the eighteenth century. He'd thrown many lavish parties there, so anyone who was aspiring to be somebody in society at the time had lived nearby. As a result, all these grand manor houses and halls had sprung up around the area. Some were lovely old houses nestled in under the beautiful rolling hills, like something out of a Jane Austen novel, while others were grossly extravagant eyesores that stuck out against the landscape, at odds with their surroundings.

Finally, at a junction in the road near Moneyash, it was time for us to part ways. I was sad to say goodbye to Janine. She was such a bright and positive person and she'd really given my mood a lift during our stay.

A few miles down the road at Parsley Hay, we picked up the Tissington Trail. It was another old railway line that ran along a high ridge, affording us views across the beautiful Derbyshire countryside with its patchwork of gently sloping fields broken here and there by rocky outcrops to which clung small, windswept hawthorn trees.

After several hours of happy wandering along the flat, deserted track, we left the trail and followed a narrow lane that dropped steeply down into Dovedale. There the road ran along the banks of the River Dove as it carved its way between high, wooded hills to the pretty village of Milldale, before climbing sharply up again to the top of a broad hill where the countryside opened up around us once more.

I was lost deep in my thoughts by now, and Taliesin was lost deep in his, so when Spirit suddenly stopped dead to sniff something neither of us noticed. For the second time on the journey, Taliesin trod on her.

Loud, gut-wrenching yelps of agony rent the otherwise silent air, startling birds from the bushes and sheep from where they dozed under stone walls in the neighbouring fields.

My heart skipped several beats.

Looking down, I saw Spirit hopping on three legs, blood streaming from her hind paw. It was the same one Taliesin had trodden on before, back up near Callander several weeks earlier.

I leapt off Taliesin to get a closer look at the damage, and found to my horror that the main pad in the middle of Spirit's paw had burst open under the full weight of Taliesin's iron-shod hoof.

Spirit was whining and crying pitifully. She pushed her nose into my hands, licking me frenziedly, desperately seeking sympathy and reassurance. It was heart-breaking to see her in so much pain. Poor old Spirit!

I comforted her as best I could, and once the initial shock had worn off, I looked around and took stock of our situation.

We were in the back of beyond, about five miles from our stop. There was not a soul in sight, and to top it off, there was no mobile phone signal to call for help. There was nothing for it. We had no choice but to push on to the next stop and assess things from there.

Spirit managed bravely, sometimes taking weight on the paw, but often hopping, and the wound dripped for the first few miles, leaving a trail of blood in our wake. My mood, which had been so bright and positive when we'd left Janine earlier that morning, had given way to an all-consuming sense of despair and hopelessness. What was I to do now? We couldn't carry on like this. Spirit wouldn't manage. She could barely walk on that paw at all! She needed to rest, but we couldn't really stop anywhere for that amount of time. Should I just call it quits, throw in the towel and go home? I didn't want to give up. We had come so far! But what else was there to do?

That night we were staying with endurance enthusiast Linda and her daughter, Lissie. Once Taliesin had been unburdened, fed, watered and turned out into a field for the night, I set about tending to Spirit's paw, which at long last had stopped bleeding. The wound looked deep and painful. All the fatty tissues that made up the pad were exposed where it had burst open in a huge split right down the middle.

It did not look good.

We were a day's ride from Cannock Chase in Staffordshire and Guy, who had helped us so much at the start of the journey, was coming up to meet us the following day.

Guy had grown up near Cannock Chase and had lived in Lichfield for many years. He still had a lot of friends in the area, so when he heard that we were heading that way he volunteered to drive up and spend a day with us. One of Guy's old schoolmates, Johnny Meakin, had kindly offered us a place to stay on his farm, and so the plan fell neatly into place. I had been really looking forward to seeing Guy again, but Spirit's accident suddenly threw the whole journey off course and into jeopardy.

'Don't panic, lovely!' Guy said reassuringly as I filled him in on the day's events over the phone that night. 'We'll work something out.'

But I was panicking. I knew Spirit couldn't carry on in this state. She needed time to rest, and time to heal. Time we simply didn't have with winter, wet weather, and the long dark evenings close on our heels.

What could I do?

I had to make a decision, and soon; but I was too down in the dumps to think straight that night so I went to bed and hoped things would look better in the morning.

They didn't.

Spirit was still walking gingerly on her bad leg, and hopping every few strides in spite of the bandage I had put on it.

Linda and Lissie offered to keep her for the day and bring her down to me that evening at the next stop. That would have been the best thing for Spirit's paw, but I knew Spirit far too well to believe that she would happily stay with two strangers while I rode off without her. Injured or not, she's an anxious creature and she has a very destructive streak. I couldn't inflict that on these lovely, kind people, not after all they had done for me!

No, there was nothing for it but to push on for one more day.

So we did. For twenty-six gruelling miles across the dull, flat Staffordshire landscape with Spirit limping bravely along beside us the whole way, and me riddled with guilt for asking her to do it.

At long last, just as the light was starting to fade and a cold rain beginning to fall, we arrived at Johnny Meakin's farm near Little Haywood on the edge of Cannock Chase.

There were acres of rich, fertilised grass, and several long sheds full of bullocks, but not a soul stirred about the place so I rang the number Guy had given me for our host. A short while later a truck pulled up and Johnny tumbled out. He was clearly fresh out of the pub. He reeked of whiskey, was slurring badly, and staggered uncertainly as he walked. But he had a good heart, and he lost no time in showing Taliesin to a field and making me a nice hot drink, before leading me and Spirit to the mobile home where we were to sleep for the next few nights.

I was just settling in when Guy arrived.

Oh, how good it was to see a familiar face again after all those weeks on the road! The last time I had seen Guy was in Durness, right at the beginning of the journey. I'd been panicking then, terrified about what lay ahead of us. Now, here we were only a few weeks away from home, and although I was calm and confident about the journey, this time I was panicking about what to do with Spirit, and worried I would have to call a premature halt to the whole thing!

'Have you spoken to Cate?' Guy asked.

I hadn't. Not properly. I was reluctant to ask for her help. She had done so much for us over the years and would never accept anything in return. I didn't want to ask this of her, it was too much. I couldn't! - could I? Cate adored Spirit, and Spirit adored Cate. Cate understood her, knew how to manage her wolf-ish, neurotic behaviour, and Cate was one of the few people with whom I could leave Spirit, happy in the knowledge that I wouldn't return to find her escaped with half the neighbourhood's cats, dogs, and livestock lying dead or injured in her wake.

After deliberating on it for a while, and finding no viable alternative, I finally and reluctantly picked up the phone and called her.

Cate didn't hesitate for so much as a second. She immediately offered to drive up to Glastonbury the following evening to meet Guy, relieve him of Spirit and take her back to Cornwall, where I knew she would spoil Spirit rotten and give her all the time and rest she needed until I returned.

'What are friends for?' she scolded, when I expressed my reservations at asking for her help. I breathed a sigh of relief. All would be well after all, and the journey would continue.

Thank God for Cate! And thank God for Guy! Without the unwavering support of those two amazing souls, the journey would not only have died an untimely death then and there, but would probably never have been possible in the first place! I have a lot to thank them for.

After a day spent catching up with many of Guy's old friends and acquaintances in and around Lichfield, the moment I had been dreading finally arrived.

I bundled Spirit into the boot of the car with all the dog food I'd had stashed in my saddle bags, gave Guy a heartfelt hug, and for the second time on that journey I watched as Guy's car pulled away into the gathering darkness.

She was gone.

I waited until red taillights of the car vanished into the night, fighting back the tears and all the misery that threatened to swallow me up. For the first time in the whole journey I felt lonely. It was a horrible feeling, accompanied by deafening, empty silence. I had never really been aware of all the comforting little noises Spirit made, never registered how much her presence had filled the space. She had been so much a part of me, and without her I felt empty.

I wandered down to the field gate and called into the darkness. There was a soft nicker and a big dark shadow moved against the blackness of the hedge. Taliesin ambled over and gently nuzzled my hand, seeking out the carrot I had brought him, as I buried my face into the thick hair of his warm neck. I wanted so badly to fetch my tent and sleep in the field with him; at least that way I wouldn't feel so utterly alone. But it was late, it was dark, and I told myself firmly that I had to get used to the silence and the emptiness.

I slept badly that night, half-alert, with one ear listening out for any unusual noises. Until that moment I hadn't realised how reassuring Spirit's presence had been, how much I relied on her as my protector to keep watch and alert me to danger, or how much companionship she had provided - not just over the last few months travelling, but in all the years that I'd had her. Without her it was just me, alone in the big world.

29

The West Midlands

It was strange setting off without Spirit the next day, but practically speaking it was a lot less stressful. There was no incessant, irritating pulling on my arm as she tried to sniff things or scent mark, and no more of the dead-stops that had landed her in such a mess, twice! Gone were the worries that she might randomly attack people's friendly and inquisitive dogs, their cats, chickens or any other livestock we encountered. Actually, apart from missing the security and the companionship she had provided, without Spirit the journey became a great deal easier.

The first few miles of the day were spent crossing Cannock Chase, a small haven of wilderness in the middle of that built up area in the north midlands, where one town appeared to flow seamlessly into the next. The hills on the Chase were clad in purple heather and dying bracken, and there were silver birch trees growing along the banks of shallow streams. It reminded me a little of Scotland, and for a short while I became absorbed in the beauty of the landscape. Then, leaving the Chase behind us, we picked up roads which led through busy towns and bustling villages in the flat, crowded countryside, and my mood became heavy and introspective again.

That night we stayed at a B&B on the outskirts of Wolverhampton. Taliesin had a field next to the aged, fat cob, who belonged to the B&B owner's daughter. Taliesin didn't seem interested in the presence of another horse, and was far more intent on throwing himself against the spindly trees that grew in his paddock for a good, vigorous scratch. They buckled and groaned under his weight. Between the midges, the mild weather and his ever-thickening winter coat, he was becoming itchier by the day!

I was given a clean and comfortable room overlooking Taliesin's paddock, and after a nice soak in a hot bath I went downstairs to see about dinner.

The owner of the B&B was a very peculiar man indeed. Short, rotund, and with skinny little legs, he put me in mind of a spinning top. His curly brown hair was thinning on top, and he had small, piggy eyes hidden behind round spectacles. When he spoke, which was often, and nearly always about himself, he rolled his 'r's in the most eccentric fashion, and accentuated everything he said with flamboyant hand gestures as he spun and twirled around the kitchen, reaching for this herb and that spice to enhance my rather simple meal of couscous and vegetables. All that tripping and twirling only added to my mental image of a spinning top. Yet in spite of his cumbersome figure, he moved lightly, carrying himself with the grace and poise of a dancer.

My host's moods were strange, too. One minute he would be cheerful and pleasant, and the next he would be cold and distant - almost angry. He flipped between the two states of being at a confusing and irrational rate, which put me quite on edge. So I tried to encourage him to talk about the one thing that seemed to keep his mood on an even, positive keel - himself. While he took centre stage I sat back and enjoyed the spectacle, doing my utmost to demonstrate appropriate levels of interest, awe and wonder, interjecting gasps and sighs, 'wow's and non-committal, yet encouraging, 'mm's into gaps in the stories he told me about the many wonderful things he'd done with his life. It was hard work, this ego-stroking, and I was glad when at last I could slip away to the solitude of my room.

The following night, we stayed with an old acquaintance of mine near Kinver.

I had realised, only days before, that Ed - whom I had known many years earlier from the community where I'd grown up - now ran a farm on the outskirts of Stourbridge. I had dropped him a message to say we were passing, and he had been more than happy to offer us shelter for a night.

The farm was owned by Ruskin Mill Trust, as part of the Glasshouse College for young people with special needs. Students from the college attended art and craft workshops throughout the week, and some worked on the farm looking after the goats, cows and chickens, and growing vegetables to supply local shops, cafes, and veg box delivery schemes. The farm itself was managed along Biodynamic principles, a method of farming that uses no chemicals, views the farm holistically, and takes into account not just the effects of the sun, moon and seasons on plants and their development, but also the influences of the other planets in our solar system. It is a method of farming first envisioned by philosopher and social reformer Rudolf Steiner in the 1920's, and has since been developed over the decades by dedicated followers of Steiner's teachings. With both my parents being staunch Anthroposophists, and having attended a Steiner school from a young age right up until I was nineteen years old, Biodynamic agriculture was no foreign concept to me. In fact, between that and growing up living alongside people with special needs, the whole set-up at Vale Head Farm was a familiar and rather homely one.

Taliesin and I had passed an easy day navigating relatively quiet lanes and bridle paths. I was mostly leading Taliesin because something had rubbed symmetrical bald patches into the hair on his back and I was worried about aggravating them by riding. An old man pushing a bicycle laden with all his worldly possessions fell into step with us for the last few miles as we approached Vale Head Farm. From the stories he told me, he had travelled a lot in his youth but now resided in Kinver. He took all his possessions with him wherever he went because, he said, he didn't trust the other people in the hostel where he lived. He was a bit of an odd sort but harmless enough, and the miles passed quickly with someone else to talk to.

When I arrived, the farm was deserted save for Folu, the young Nigerian man who was doing his Biodynamic apprenticeship there. Folu showed Taliesin to a field, and then took me up to the packing shed where he was sorting the stacks of freshly harvested vegetables into boxes ready for delivery in the morning.

Folu, an artist and musician, was pleasant company, and he was more than happy to let me sample the vast array of fresh, brightly coloured vegetables. There were peppers, tomatoes, carrots, onions, beetroots, leeks, cabbage, celeriac, potatoes, spinach, chard, lettuce, and squash of all shapes and sizes, and that was only the half of it! Living off a staple diet of pasta, rice and couscous for the last two months, I went weak at the knees before this colourful abundance of nourishing goodness. It was a vegan heaven! Who knew vegetables could be so exciting? And thus we passed the time cheerfully, with Folu working hard, and me feasting unashamedly on the harvest, until Ed arrived.

It was strange seeing Ed after all those years. I was little more than ten or eleven years old when he had spent a few months working in the Camphill Community one summer. The tangle of long, dark dreadlocks, which I remembered so vividly, had vanished. In their place was short-cropped hair, now grey, but the bright blue eyes were the same, and the smile.

I had been a bit of an odd child - saying that, I'm probably a bit of an odd adult too - and back then I hadn't really liked people. I remember, to my shame, that I certainly hadn't liked Ed. So much so that I'd once poured salt - or was it sugar? – into his water bottle on a hot summer's day when he'd left it unattended in the barn.

Fortunately for me, Ed didn't remember that episode, and so offered me some warm hospitality for the evening in the home that he shared with his partner, Carolina, and their two lovely young children, Rosa and Leon. After the children had gone to bed we sat up chatting over a pot of herb tea, reminiscing about many of the characters we'd known in Camphill and discussing the demise of those communities, not just in the UK but all across the world. Their unique approach to living and working – life-sharing! - with people with disabilities was rapidly vanishing, drowning in a sea of bureaucracy and red tape. It had been more than a mere 'job' to people such as my parents, more than support work or care work. For many who had dedicated their lives to it, it had been a true vocation and it was sad to see that under attack in today's unforgiving and intolerant world. Many of the residents in Camphill Communities had themselves once been students at Ruskin Mill, and I was glad to find that Ruskin Mill's approach to working with young adults with disabilities was still thriving.

When at last I turned in for the night, I slept deeply. It was the first time I'd done so since Spirit's departure. That was a wonderful stay. Vale Head Farm really was a special place.

30

The Missing Link

As you may have gathered from previous chapters, I am not a great fan of bridleways. I have been let down by too many, I find them to be more hassle than they're worth, and anyone who waxes lyrical about how wonderful they are has clearly never tried to navigate from one end of the country to the other using the bloody things.

Saying that, however, we had actually had a good run of them since the last fiasco back in Lancashire on the day that Taliesin fell into the bog. What with the Pennine Bridleway and all those old railway lines, the going had been rather good. Thanks to that my guard was down, my confidence was at an all time high, and I had become woefully complacent about adding bridleways into our daily route without a second thought or a back-up plan.

I suppose it was inevitable, then, that something had to go wrong.

With only ten miles to cover on the day we left Vale Head Farm, I'd decided to spend the morning helping out about the place; feeding the goats, mending some fencing, and chatting to the students and their support workers about our journey. The atmosphere at Vale Head was so warm, welcoming, and peaceful that I found myself very reluctant to leave. It was like a quiet haven from the world at large, a place out of time. I would have loved to stay on for a day or two longer and bask in the beautiful atmosphere, but stops had been arranged and people were expecting us, so we had to push on.

We were heading towards the River Severn, which we needed to cross in order to bypass some of the large towns and busy roads that made up Birmingham's urban sprawl. My map showed only one logical route between Vale Head Farm and our next stop near Stottesdon: a bridleway that went right through the middle of the Severn Valley Country Park, crossing the river by way of a foot bridge. There was no other bridge over the river for several miles in either direction, and all alternatives involved a lengthy detour on busy roads, which would add both miles and hours onto our day.

I had plotted the route carefully, pleased - smug even - to have found a bridleway which for once was right where we needed it to be, and actually went somewhere useful. I was delighted, too, by the prospect of another short day for Taliesin. Life was good, the odds were in our favour, and my mood was positively chirpy!

So you can imagine my dismay when, on reaching the spot where the bridleway should have been, I found no bridleway. Instead, there was a drive leading down to a stable yard. I wondered briefly whether this was one of those oh-so-common bridleways that isn't actually signposted and recognisable only to locals, so I flagged down a woman who was pulling out of the drive and asked her. When she assured me that we would definitely not find a way into the country park through the stable yard, my heart sank a little.

'Here we go!' I thought to myself.

'Try the next lane along,' she said. 'If you follow it right down through the trading estate, you can get into the park that way.'

I relaxed a little. False alarm. No need to panic!

So we traipsed all the way down through the long industrial estate, right to very the bottom of the hill, and sure enough there was the entrance into the country park. And just beyond it, was the bridge over the Severn! But blocking our path were two solid, metal A-frame barriers with no way around them. Wide at the bottom and narrow at the top, the barriers were made in such a way as to allow walkers and cyclists to pass through, but not vehicles – and not horse riders either!

I examined the barriers closely. Taliesin might just be able to squeeze through if he wasn't wearing a saddle and packs, I thought. The woman had seemed pretty certain we could get into the park this way. As a local, and a horse rider, surely she must know. It was worth a try!

So I tied Taliesin up and bit by bit removed his packs, saddle and blankets, lugged them through the barriers, and piled them all up on the other side. Then I went to fetch Taliesin. He ambled willingly up to the barriers, eager to attempt whatever I asked of him, took a step forward and stopped dead. He couldn't do it. He was just that little bit too wide, and that tiny bit too tall to squeeze through, and no matter how hard he tried - and try he did - he just couldn't do it.

I cursed.

Tying Taliesin up again, I had to lug all the gear back through the barriers and spent twenty minutes or so tacking him back up and loading all the packs onto the saddle once more. Then, still muttering curses, we plodded all the way back up the hill, out of the trading estate and turned down the drive into the stable yard where my map said the bridleway ought to be.

'No,' the people on the yard said flatly, eyeing us up with deep suspicion, 'there's no bridleway here. Never has been.'

My map said otherwise, but it was no use arguing.

We could get into the country park if we retraced our steps back into the village of Alveley and turned down another road signposted for the country park, one lady eventually offered, but she didn't think I could get into Highly from there with a horse.

This was not promising. I needed to get into Highly for our onward route and I didn't have time now to take a detour in order to find another way across the river. Time and daylight were no longer on our side.

We trudged wearily back up the drive, retracing our steps into Alveley. All the peace and happiness I'd felt at Vale Head Farm that morning had long since vanished and I was now in a foul mood.

At long last we found ourselves in the park, on the footbridge, and on the right side of the barriers. The black cloud of irritation lifted for a moment as we finally crossed the river. The moment was short-lived though, because when I stopped to ask a dog walker which of the many criss-crossing tracks would bring us out in Highly, she looked at us doubtfully and said there were barriers or gates at the end of all the tracks, and there definitely wasn't a bridleway up to the village.

Well, I decided, bridleway or no bridleway we were getting out of this accursed country park and into Highly one way or another. We had come too far to turn back and I was in no mood for much more of this nonsense!

We struck out along the track that my map said should have been the bridleway. It brought us up to a small steam railway line where there was a gated crossing. According to my map, the bridleway crossed the railway there and continued on to the village. But on the gates of the crossing was a sign saying 'strictly no horses'.

I'd had enough by this point. Signs be damned! I was crossing here whether people liked it or not! So we did, and eventually we came to the end of a track where there was a gate, and luckily for the gate, the country park, my frayed nerves, and my rapidly vanishing sanity, it was big enough to accommodate Taliesin, packs and all. We squeezed through and at long last found ourselves in Highly.

I was glad to leave the park behind us, and relieved when the other bridleways we were counting on that day were exactly where they were meant to be and went where they were supposed to and I vowed that never again would I rely on a bridleway for anything!

31

Twenty-Seven

It was the fourteenth of October, my twenty-seventh birthday, and I was having a good day.

Birthdays are meant to be a joyous occasion, a cause for celebration, but in recent years they had become a rather depressing affair in which I usually found myself wondering where the year had gone, what I'd managed to achieve in it, and what exactly I was doing with my life. Upon finding that I had achieved nothing and was still no closer to realising my dreams than I had been the year before, I would become quite depressed and miserable at the thought that time was slipping quietly by, while I procrastinated my life away in an uncomfortable but familiar little rut.

That had been the general way of things for most birthdays in my twenties, but this time things were different. Here I was, nearly at the end of the epic horseback journey I'd been dreaming of since my childhood. And what a truly incredible experience it had been so far! What people we had met, what challenges faced, and what odds we had overcome! Yes, this year at last, progress had been made!

It was a warm, sunny day and only a handful of clouds drifted across bright blue skies. I was riding Taliesin bareback because Jane, who had hosted us for the last two nights, had kindly offered to drop our things on to the next stop. I was grateful for the offer because it would give Taliesin's back a bit of a break. Things beneath the saddle as usual weren't looking too good. It seemed that the moment one lot of lumps disappeared, others would come up somewhere else; and a few days earlier, I had noticed two symmetrical bald patches where the hair had rubbed out completely.

We meandered quietly along peaceful lanes, dipping down into shallow valleys and climbing small rises in the landscape as we made our steady way towards the Malvern hills, whose large contours rose up suddenly out of the otherwise flat landscape ahead of us.

I treated myself to lunch at a pub and sat out in the beer garden, basking in the warm October sunshine while Taliesin grazed happily between the tables. Every now and then, when he thought I wasn't looking, he would make a beeline for the rickety old climbing frame in the corner to scratch one of his many itches. I would have to intervene, then, because I knew he'd knock the whole lot over.

Nearing the hills, we passed acres of sleepy orchards. Farmyards filled with enormous heaps of harvested apples, and trailers piled high with ripe fruit lay baking in the warm sunshine. The sweet smell of apples hung heavy in the still air. The hedgerows were laden with red hawthorn and rowan berries, and great clumps of mistletoe grew in the tall oak and ash trees that bordered the lanes. Beneath them, the fallen leaves created a rustling carpet of yellows, browns and reds under Taliesin's hooves.

Then up over the Malverns we went, in one long, breathless ascent, followed by a steep descent the other side, arriving at last at our stop for the night - a field in Welland where Ellen kept her little herd of equines.

Ellen Cochrane is a gifted horsewoman, with a passion for working with horses in a gentle, respectful way. Her focus lies on developing strong communication with horses through positive reinforcement and the subtle use of body language. She can frequently be seen riding with neither saddle nor bridle, yet her horses are as biddable as any trained using more conventional methods. If the black-boots-and-white-jodhpurs brigade is at one end of the equestrian spectrum, then this compassionate, soft approach to working in partnership with horses is what lies at the other.

I knew Ellen through the organisation upon whose website I had discovered Taliesin and Oisín all those years ago. Ellen had rescued a French Trotter mare a few months before I had acquired my two feral foals. It melted my heart to think how far Taliesin had come in the eight years since he and Oisín had arrived. Back then, I had only dreamt of what strong and noble horses they would become; willing partners to me on my mad adventures, and the makers of my wildest dreams. Then I thought with sadness of all the other horses that had never been given the chance to show their potential or prove their worth. Of the fifteen foals on that site looking for homes, only three had made it out alive.

That evening I went out to dinner with Alan Sheppard, an aspiring equestrian traveller. He was planning to ride a horse around France the following year and wanted to pick my brains about equipment and all the finer details of horseback travel - which is probably my favourite topic of conversation. And so a wonderful day turned into a wonderful evening.

Later that night, as I lay in my tent next to Taliesin's paddock listening to the sound of him munching his steady way through a pile of haylage and thinking back over the year just gone, I concluded that finally I was exactly where I wanted to be, doing what I'd always wanted to do, and that life was pretty good. It had been an excellent birthday. The best I'd had in years!

32

Saddle Sores and the Problem with Planning

The following night, we stayed with Long Rider William Reddaway.

In 2013, at the age of sixty-five, William set out with his horse, Strider, to ride 2,700 miles around the four corners of England, visiting thirty cathedrals along the way in a journey that took him seven months to complete. He had contacted me several weeks earlier to offer us accommodation on our way through Cheltenham.

I was apprehensive about meeting William. I had read about his journey, and from the little correspondence we'd had, I had formed the impression that he was a bit of a stickler for good preparation, organisation, and punctuality. I feared that he'd think me terribly disorganised, with my haphazard approach to route planning, lackadaisical attitude to finding stops and rather vague estimated times of arrival.

My apprehension about our meeting only grew when, on nearing our destination, I slid down from Taliesin's enormous heights, removed the saddlecloth, and found to my horror that he had two hot, hard swellings on his back where the bald patches had been. On one side, the skin was actually broken. I was mortified. This was exactly what I had been trying to avoid by riding bareback that day!

Alan Sheppard had very kindly offered to drive my things over to William's, and I had agreed. It would be nice for Taliesin to have another day without either a saddle or packs. I had, however, decided to keep my saddle pad in order to make the riding more comfortable for me. It was a thick pad made of canvas, and filled with a layer of fine cork filings, rather like a beanbag. The idea was that it would even out any pressure under the saddle and help prevent saddle sores. I had bought it especially for the ride. But throughout the course of the day, the cork in the pad had shifted downwards to form hard, compact lumps against Taliesin's sides, which had then caused the very thing the pad was supposed to prevent: pressure. Maybe this was the reason why Taliesin had suffered an inexplicable series of lumps and bumps under the saddle for the last few weeks!

William was waiting for us at the top of Nottingham Hill when we arrived, puffing and panting after a steep climb. Far from being the stern and judgemental person I had imagined, I found William to be a kind man. He was warm and welcoming, and as a horseback traveller himself, he knew our needs without asking or being asked. Taliesin was first offered water to drink, then turned out in an enormous field. A short while later, when he'd had time to explore his surroundings, roll, relax, and sample the grass, he was given a good feed. Next, we sorted through my things, piled everything I needed for the night into the back of William's car, and off we went to his house in Cheltenham where a hot bath and delicious dinner awaited us. What followed was a splendid evening spent with William and his lovely wife, Christine. Time flew as we looked over my onward route and shared stories from the road. All my apprehension melted away as William recounted the many difficulties he'd encountered on his own adventures, from missing or impassable bridleways, to the saddle sores which had seen him walk for 1,000 miles while Strider's back recovered. My problems on the road paled in comparison and made my journey seem like a walk in the park. Strider sounded like a real character and full of quirks, which made for excellent stories but tough travelling. Between escaping in the middle of the night on more than one occasion, to maintaining a strong aversion to wheelie bins even after nearly 3,000 miles, he made Taliesin look like a saint worth his weight in gold. As if I didn't already know!

But my initial assumption that William was a fastidious planner and rigid timekeeper hadn't been so very far off the mark. William had spent many months meticulously planning every step of his journey. He'd arranged each stop for the entire duration of the ride before he even set off, and had sent out packages containing the maps and changes of clothing that he'd need. It was like a well-executed military operation. What he hadn't allowed for with all that planning was things going awry with his horse - which they inevitably did. Half way through his journey, arriving at the home of our mutual acquaintances the Towneleys, he discovered to his dismay that Strider had developed saddle sores so severe he'd had to be rested for ten days, after which William had been forced to continue on foot. That unexpected break had scuppered his onward plans when some of his hosts could no longer accommodate him at a later date.

When it comes to horseback travel, anything can happen and it's no good working to too rigid a schedule. Perhaps my rather laid back, flexible approach wasn't such a bad thing after all!

33

Hurricane Ophelia

The trouble with having an unflappable horse is that even when you're trudging across the open hilltops in the midst of a howling gale, and your map comes loose from its case and gets blown away right under said horse's nose, that horse doesn't so much as bat an eyelid or give any kind of signal that something is amiss. By the time you realise that you are without a map in unfamiliar territory, with a good twenty miles to cover to your next stop, your map is well and truly lost beyond retrieval.

That was the predicament in which I found myself half way across Cleeve Common, about ten minutes after bidding William a fond farewell.

Hurricane Ophelia had swept in off the Atlantic overnight and was raging wildly, but the wind was warm and the day dry. The sun was out, burning through a thick, yellow atmosphere, and it hung like a dull, orange-red ball in the sky above us.

My stomach hit the floor and my heart stopped mid beat when, reaching for my map case to check our bearings, I found it empty. If there was one thing on which I had been relying on this journey, it was my maps. I looked again, in disbelief. Definitely still no maps!

Why had Taliesin not reacted? Any normal horse would have had a complete meltdown about the flapping map case, never mind a bloody great bit of paper flying out from under his nose.

Once I'd recovered from the shock, I laughed. Oh well. It was an interesting turn of events and yet another obstacle to overcome, but I had dealt with worse. I was in possession of a fully charged mobile phone with GPS features, several good mapping systems including the Ordnance Survey app, and I had enough 4G signal to download the very map which I had just lost - all for less than £2. In the grand scheme of things, losing my maps was barely even a hiccough. A year earlier, such an occurrence would probably have sent me into a blind panic, but months on the road had taught me to be both relaxed and resourceful in a crisis. I had learnt to trust that things were rarely as bad as they seemed and that a solution was never far off, if only you remained calm enough to find it.

We descended from the windswept common and picked our way through the suburbs of Cheltenham, stopping for coffee and supplies at a little corner shop. All the passers-by stopped to gawp at the unusual spectacle of a woman leading a horse through the town. Some came over to chat, but not many. In these parts people kept themselves to themselves and merely shot us sidelong glances of thinly veiled curiosity. Without a saddle and all our gear, we looked far less like travel weary adventurers and much more like a woman who had taken leave of her senses and was taking her horse for a stroll around town as one might a dog!

As we pushed on, the sky became black. Daylight faded to a dusk-like half-light as though night were falling, yet it was barely midday. Fearing a torrential downpour, I suddenly regretted leaving my waterproofs in the back of William's car that morning along with all the other things he was going to drop over to our next stop. But the rain never came and soon the darkness lifted again to reveal that strange, orange sun, watery against the murky haze.

We had been very lucky with the weather, having been soaked through no more than four times in nearly eight weeks. Considering that 2017 was widely acknowledged to have been one of the wettest, most miserable summers we'd had in years, I didn't think that was bad going at all! It seemed that wherever we went, we just so happened to be in the only dry part of the entire country. Luck had been on our side.

That night, we were staying at the Red Horse Foundation on the outskirts of Stroud. It was a centre for Equine Assisted Therapy, and unlike the RDA its focus was less on the physical benefits of horse riding, and more on how horses can be used for psychotherapy, personal growth, and learning.

Their approach to therapy worked on the principle that horses, as highly sensitive herd animals, are finely tuned to reading and responding to even the subtlest of changes in their environment and the body language and behaviour of those around them. The horse, therefore, can act as a mirror to the human, reacting to and reflecting back the mental and emotional states of the people around them. By working with both a horse and a trained therapist, clients can quickly identify emotional issues, learn to recognise patterns of behaviour, and then work to overcome them. Although a relatively new technique in therapeutic circles, equine assisted psychotherapy is a fast growing form of treatment due its ability to produce profound, effective results in a much shorter time frame than other, more conventional methods.

That night I slept in the on-site yurt, bedding down in front of the wood-burner and listening to the now gentle wind rustling through the leaves of the hazel and linden trees outside. I watched a star through the roof window, a pinprick of silver-blue light against a dark sky, as the flickering glow of the fire brought alive the paintings of primeval horses that lined the walls. A shadow moved in the firelight and the little tabby yard cat, who had crept in under the canvas at the back of the yurt, came padding quietly across the floor and climbed onto my lap. He settled down beside me for a while, on the pile of sheepskins and woollen blankets that made up my bed, purring loudly. Outside, I could hear Taliesin's heavy footfalls as he moved in the paddock behind the yurt, the steady ripping and chewing as he munched on mouthfuls of grass and hay. There was something about falling asleep in front of a crackling fire, listening to the wind beyond the thin canvas walls and watching the distant stars with my horse grazing close by that resonated deep within me, like an old memory; an echo of an ancient, timeless world. This was a moment out of time. I didn't want to let go of that feeling.

34

Glastonbury

Leaving the Red Horse Foundation, we spent the day zig-
zagging our way into deep valleys and climbing the long, steep
hills on the other side. We then found ourselves meandering
along narrow lanes for several miles, past arable fields, pasture, and
patches of native woodland until the valleys became shallower and the
land eventually levelled out to flat, cow-grazed commons as we
approached our stop - a livery yard at Wapley. I noticed suddenly how
short the days were becoming now, with dusk falling early and dawn
coming late. It was still dark when I got up at seven. Winter would
soon be upon us and back in the Highlands there had already been
snow.

The next day we travelled through Bath. It had been the easiest
option to get across the seemingly impassable band of urban sprawl
that stretched from Bristol all the way to Devizes. Here one town
seemed to flow into the next with barely a break in between, all
threaded through with many busy roads.

We were on the west side of Bath where there were no bridleways
and no easy way to cross the river Avon. At first we navigated the
quiet back streets of the suburbs, before making full, but probably
illegal, use of pavements and pedestrian crossings to manoeuvre our
way through the unavoidable trunk roads leading into the city centre.

Taliesin moved placidly amongst traffic, unperturbed by the noisy engines, blaring horns, and the screaming sirens. He followed me trustingly along those chaotic streets until at long last we reached quiet country lanes once more.

I was walking, and Taliesin still carried no gear. With careful planning, the help of some friends in Stroud and the legendary Guy, who had yet again come to the rescue in my hour of need, I managed to get from Stroud to Glastonbury carrying nothing but a small rucksack with a toothbrush, a bottle of water, some snacks, and a change of underwear.

We stopped on the outskirts of Bath that night. I was in a B&B and Taliesin stayed in a field offered to us by Anne, a long-standing volunteer at the Wellow RDA group.

From there, we made for Wells and got a good soaking in the relentless rain that poured for much of the day. Not a bit of me remained dry, but I was in a cheerful mood all the same. I would be spending the night at Guy's house in Glastonbury. A bath, hot meal, dry clothes, and comfy bed awaited me!

The rain eased off in the late afternoon, just as we crested the southern escarpment of the Mendip Hills. The Somerset levels opened up before us, flat, save for the handful of scattered hills which rose out of the plain like islands from a lake. And there, in the middle of it, with its dark stone tower set against a backdrop of shifting grey rain clouds, stood Glastonbury Tor - that place steeped in magic, myth and legend. My breath caught in my throat. It was the first familiar view I had seen in a very long time! We were in home territory now, on the last leg of the journey.

I felt sad suddenly as the reality hit me that in just over a week's time I would be back in Cornwall and this journey would be over. I didn't want it to end and I didn't want to go home, back to 'normality' and a mundane existence. Out here on the road I had never felt so alive, so switched on and connected, both to the land and to the people in it. Moving quietly through the gradually shifting landscapes and the changing seasons, experiencing in intricate detail the progression of each as we wandered at our slow and steady pace across the country, under the boundless skies.

148

We came down from the Mendips, following a small, winding lane into the village of Easton. Ahead of us on a pavement stood a signpost. The metal pole was painted black and it had one arm, pointing to the east. 'A371 Wells 3 miles'. There was something familiar about that signpost. I had seen it before. I had been here before. A year earlier we had passed this very spot - Taliesin, Oisín, Spirit and I - on our little, but oh-so-difficult 300-mile journey around the South West. This was the point where all my journeys converged. When I reached it, I would - over several years, on three different adventures and with two different horses - have ridden from one end of Britain to the other. It was only a signpost, a meaningless inanimate object, but something stirred in me all the same and I had to fight back tears.

Even in Taliesin some distant memory seemed to awaken, a faint hint of recognition, because when we arrived at Redmond Bottom Livery Yard where he had stayed the year before with Oisín, he suddenly became unsettled and uncharacteristically clingy, calling for me as I walked away down the drive to await Guy's arrival. Hearing him neigh with such frantic desperation and confusion in his voice melted my heart. I may not have wanted to go home, but Taliesin needed to. He missed his herd, especially Oisín with whom he had shared so much over the years. He had done his work, and courageously too. He deserved a good, long rest. Yes, for all my misgivings, it was time to go home.

We spent the next day crossing the Somerset Levels on flat, straight roads that ran parallel to deep ditches full of stagnant water, lined with tall willow trees. I walked mostly, and every now and then I rode a little, careful not to let my legs touch Taliesin's sides where the sore was healing well. I had walked 100 miles in five days, no wonder my body ached! It is amazing what you can do when needs must. I had come to realise on this journey that stamina has very little to do with physical strength and fitness, and far more to do with mind-set and determination.

We were staying at Burrow Bridge for a few nights. Again, Taliesin was in a place where he had been the year before. Cheryl Green, who kept a small herd of competition horses, hadn't hesitated in offering Taliesin accommodation for the second year in a row.

I was staying with my friend April just down the road, in her tiny open plan flat on the second floor of an old converted barn. April is an ex-cabaret singer, West End chorus girl, and musician of many talents. I had met her several years earlier through the band, and while at first I had found her to be chaotic and disorganised, I soon discovered that under that mad, scatty, colourful exterior, lay a heart of pure gold. She was like an older sister, deeply empathic, intuitive, willing to listen with an impartial and non-judgmental ear, and always happy to advise. She had lived life to the full in her forty-odd years and could always offer the most profound insights into love, life and the ways of the Universe. A wiser, more beautiful soul you could not wish to meet - just so long as you accepted her with all her accompanying chaos!

And chaos was what awaited me at April's flat, because not only was I staying with her that weekend, but four others were as well. People were descending from all corners of the country for the Sahmain Faerie Ball in Glastonbury, and April's was an open house.

It was dark, crowded, and noisy. A heaving mass of people in brightly coloured, extravagant costumes filled the room. They were leaping, spinning, dancing and twirling to the over-powering loud music that was blaring out through the speakers at the side of the stage where a band was playing. It was funny to think that in a previous life, only a few years before, it had been me up on that stage playing to this same crowd. It was different being this side of the lights. I didn't like it. It was hot, sticky, and claustrophobic.

Everywhere I looked there were fauns and faeries, mermaids and green men, knights and ladies, witches and wizards, and just about everything in between. I dodged through the dizzying array of wings, masks, and bobbing headdresses draped in fairy lights and lashings of multi-coloured glitter; reaching the back doors of the hall, I burst out into the cool night air. I could breathe again. What a strange and heady contrast this was to all the long months of space and silence.

It was uncomfortable being in that room full of noisy chaos. I felt out of place, suffocated, and more isolated than I had felt in all the hundreds of solitary miles I had traversed with my faithful animals over the past eight weeks.

The journey had been intense, raw and brutally honest. In contrast, this all felt superficial, false and hollow. The extravagant costumes, the noise, the alcohol-fuelled revelry, and the wildly inflated egos which crowded that hot and airless room - it was all too much to stomach after the slow, silently contemplative world in which I had existed for the last two months.

I knew a few people in the crowd, and tried to make idle chit-chat, but my heart wasn't in it and I was glad when at last we left.

35

The Conquest Centre

Taliesin seemed happy to be on the move again when, after two days rest, we left April. I didn't think he'd enjoyed his time off all that much, and in return for Cheryl's generous hospitality he had broken a rail on her sand school fence with his vigorous scratching. When access to that had been denied with a strand of electric tape, he had proceeded to carve out an enormous hole in the hedge by the road. Another day and I think he'd have escaped the field altogether!

Taliesin was wearing a saddle, carrying the packs, and I was riding him for the first time in over a week. The sore on his back had healed nicely, and without the troublesome, beanbag-like saddle pad there was nothing to aggravate it again. Most of the other lumps and bumps had faded, and a fine smattering of new hair was coming through where the bald patches of skin had been.

We had a short day travelling through the flat Somerset countryside, and that night we stayed at the Conquest Centre on the outskirts of Taunton.

The Conquest Centre is a charitable organisation that offers a wide range of equine assisted therapies, from RDA accredited riding and carriage driving, to equine assisted psychotherapy and behavioural therapy. What interested me most of all was that they also offered the Horse Boy Method.

Named after the book he wrote about his journey on horseback across Mongolia in search of healing for his severely autistic son, the Horse Boy Method was developed by Rupert Isaacson specifically for children with autism. Noticing that his son, Rowan, had a strong affinity with animals and nature, both of which had a profoundly calming effect on the young child, Rupert began to take Rowan riding. He found that when in the saddle, not only was Rowan calmer and more relaxed, but that in certain gaits his non-verbal son became suddenly able to communicate fluently. Years of work followed, and with the help of both scientists and people with autism, the Horse Boy Method was developed.

The technique involves a qualified instructor sitting behind the child in the saddle, or otherwise long-reining the horse from the ground, and working it in collected gaits. The rhythmic movement of the horse acts on the child's nervous system, helping to block the stress hormone, cortisol, and release oxytocin, the feel-good hormone responsible for bonding and communication. The method works as an effective tool for helping the child to relax and feel calm, while also promoting communication and learning.

I had read the book several years earlier, and it had quickly become a firm favourite. I was touched by the story and captivated by the idea that horses could have such a profound and healing effect on people, especially young children struggling to cope in our over-stimulatory, over-sensory world.

I had heard on my travels that the Conquest Centre was deemed somewhat too radical by the RDA; their methods too controversial, too alternative. Nevertheless, I was inspired by what I saw, finding their ethos refreshing and their approach to therapy innovative.

I bedded down that night in front of a warm fire in the yurt, where the centre ran a small Forest School, while Taliesin spent the night in an open-sided stable in the big covered barn. He had a full net of hay to keep him occupied and a deep bed of straw, but rather than eating the nice, sweet hay, he opted instead to munch his way through the dusty bedding which made him cough badly, and he sweated profusely even though the walls of the stable only came as high as his shoulder.

36

The Final Days

The last few days passed in a blur as each unwilling step brought us nearer to the end of our journey. I didn't want it to be over, wasn't ready to go back to reality. Life on the road was simple, stripped back to the basics and the bare necessities. All I had to worry about each day was getting safely from one stop to the next, and finding food, water, and shelter for me and my horse. Everything else was of little consequence. The cares and worries of 'normal' existence - work, bills, rent, tax, the mundaneness of traffic jams, or a trip to the supermarket - had no relevance here. All that mattered was my horse, the weather, the open road, and the beautiful people we met along the way. This, surely, was normality!

Out here there was all the time in the world to reflect, to contemplate, to dream! There was calm and there was quiet. Nothing hurried, nothing hectic, and always the steady rhythm of Taliesin's hoof-beats, lulling me into a half-sleep state.

But that would soon vanish, and I would be sucked back into the stress and anxiety of the rat-race and the modern world. I felt like I was walking into a cage, with my eyes wide open. Soon my wings would be clipped, the cage door closed behind me, and all that serenity and silence would be swept away by the encroaching tide of financial worries and the tedious responsibilities of a shallow, meaningless existence.

I dragged my feet. Every part of me wanted to turn around and head north, back up into the wild, empty expanses of the Highlands.

I tried not to think about it. I couldn't turn around. Taliesin needed a rest, I reminded myself, and I wanted to see Spirit and my other horses again. So I forced myself onward, refusing to think about what lay ahead, focusing instead on the landscape around me.

The flat Somerset Levels had given way to gently undulating countryside at the foot of the Quantock hills, which grew, building slowly, to become huge, rolling hills as we approached Exmoor.

There were steep descents into deep, wooded valleys where ancient stone bridges crossed fast-flowing rivers that wound and tumbled their way southwards. Then long, breathless climbs along narrow, sheltered lanes to the tops of enormous hills before the next descent began. Pretty thatched cottages with picture-perfect gardens and roses growing round the door lay scattered across acres of open farmland and the people here in the West Country were warm and friendly. It was an open friendliness, the kind we'd not encountered since leaving Scotland so many weeks before.

We stayed near the old market town of Dulverton one night, at the house of Lisa Walker whom I had met on my travels the year before in Dorset. She would be moving to Exmoor, she had said, and we would be more than welcome to stay if ever we were passing that way. So I had taken her up on her kind offer, and although she wasn't at home her mother and stepfather were, and they made me feel very welcome that night with a hearty meal, a hot bath, and an enormous, comfortable bed. Taliesin was happy too, in his field full of grass next door to two of Lisa's rescued horses, her buck-toothed llama called Tony, and Billy the goat.

The next day we crossed over into Devon and retraced our steps from the year before following a dull road, which ran for miles along the top of a long ridge - stretching from the busy A361 all the way to Chulmleigh. Half way along it, we met a lorry carrying a digger. It pulled in and stopped, leaving us just enough room to slip through. At the same moment a car came flying up behind us like a bat out of hell, squeezed past without slowing down, and squealed to a halt just short of the lorry when the young man behind the wheel suddenly realised he couldn't get by.

I looked on with amusement as the lorry driver turned off his engine, climbed slowly down from the cab, strolled over to the car window, and proceeded very calmly and quietly to deliver the most patronising lecture on how to drive sensibly around horses to the red-faced driver. As we passed them, I thanked the lorry driver profusely on behalf of horse riders everywhere and was pleasantly surprised when the car overtook us slowly and respectfully a few minutes later.

That night we stayed with Emma Bowyer, an equine behaviourist with a passion for western riding and equestrian travel. She had made several short journeys with her horse over the years. It was all she could manage with a husband, a young child, and her business to run. We passed a splendid evening discussing equestrian travel and the Long Riders who had inspired us with their incredible journeys. For a while I forgot that my own Long Ride would soon be little more than a memory.

37

The End of the Road

It was Friday the 27th of October and the final day of the journey. Nine weeks to the day, and a thousand miles since Taliesin, Spirit and I had set out from Durness.

That seemed like a lifetime ago now.

I was on the road early, heading away from our final, lovely host, Sarah Dawe. Sarah had a big heart, adored her animals, and had quit her successful, high-flying career in order to start up her own business selling the organic, herbal grooming products that she had developed. They were specifically designed for horses with skin conditions such as sweet-itch, and so far had been proven effective in all the trials, including against those infernal Scottish midges!

The product, called Goodbye Flys, promised to be a real lifesaver for the thousands of horses across the country that suffered with sweet-itch and she gave me some to use on Taliesin, who even now at the end of October was still being bothered by the midges. He had no mane left and very little tail after months of vigorous, self-destructive rubbing.

I wished I had met Sarah on the first night of the journey, when we were camped at Cashel Dhu and had been eaten alive by the miserable creatures, rather than on the last!

The morning of that final day had dawned clear and bright. The sky was a rich azure blue, dotted here and there with cotton-wool clouds, and sunshine fell through the sparsely clad branches of the trees. Although warm, the air held a bite.

We wandered quietly along Devon's winding, hedge-flanked lanes that dipped and climbed through wooded valleys past little farms. Ahead and to our left rose Dartmoor, its barren tors and treacherous bogs lying placid in the late October sunshine.

Cresting the brow of a hill near Milton Abbot, the land suddenly dropped away below us. I could see Brentor, its iconic little church perched on top of a jagged, rocky outcrop, set against the sweeping backdrop of Dartmoor's brown hillsides. Ahead of us stood Kit Hill and its tall chimney stack, a relic of Cornwall's rich mining history; here, too, was my first glimpse of Bodmin moor and the skyline I knew so well.

At one end was Caradon Hill, its mast, tall and needle-like, disappearing into a bed of drifting white cloud, like a great beacon guiding me homewards. To the right rose Stowe's Hill, where Cheesewring quarry was gouged deep into the hillside, a gaping scar in the landscape; then a long sweep up to the angular granite outcrop of Sharptor and to the right of that, Bearah, Kilmar, and Hawks tors on Twelve Men's Moor lay like the rough, scaly backs of sleeping dragons. Beyond them in the far distance, Brown Willy and Rough Tor rose out of the bleak, boggy moorland.

I knew these hills, each one unique in its character, timeless and oh so familiar! I remembered how, when I first moved to Cornwall seven years earlier, that skyline had made my heart leap with excitement. Somewhere, nestled in the deep valleys at the foot of those rough slopes, in a field by a river, was the cosy little caravan I called home.

My heart sank. I didn't want to be there.

The narrow lane meandered steadily down a long and gentle slope into a valley, and eventually we arrived at Horsebridge where, crossing the River Tamar, we found ourselves back in Cornwall.

We had only a few more miles to go.

Taliesin suddenly lifted his head, pricked his ears, and picked up the pace just a fraction. After a thousand miles of unknown roads and unfamiliar territory, a spark of recognition flickered. Could it be...?

There was no big finish line to cross. Our destination was simply a field on the outskirts of Bray Shop where my other horses had spent the autumn growing fat and feral on six acres of lush grass. There was no welcoming party to greet us, no crowd gathered to cheer our arrival. There was just the one friend whom I had asked to come and meet us in order to drive me, and my belongings, the last three miles from the field back home.

And so our journey ended, quietly and without ado.

I felt no overwhelming sense of achievement as I dismounted at the field gate and, for the last time, unloaded the gear from Taliesin's broad back before letting him into the field to be reunited with his long-lost friends once more. What I felt instead was emptiness, displacement, and a sense of loss, grieving for the journey now finished.

In the weeks that followed our return I was once again reunited with Spirit - who had made a full recovery thanks to Cate's careful nursing - and I was delighted to be made a member of the Long Riders' Guild, realising yet another of my childhood dreams, but the whole experience of the journey inevitably began to fade. The raw intensity and the heightened sensation of being truly, vibrantly alive and connected to the world around me slipped quietly away, as I slowly began to switch off and shut down, drifting back into ordinary life. Sometimes it felt as though the journey had never happened, never been real.

But when I look at Taliesin, go to bury my face in his soft, shaggy winter coat, breathe in the musky odours of dried earth, hay, and sweat, and throw my arms around his thick, sturdy neck, something passes between us; a look, a feeling - a silent acknowledgement and understanding. He knows what we went through out there in the beautiful, wild mountains of the Highlands, the windswept hills of the bleak Pennines, the flat levels, the deep, wooded river valleys, and the creeping suburbs of the busy towns. He had been with me every step of the way. Nothing could take that away from us.

I might have saved his life once, but he had changed mine forever. My courageous Taliesin, my faithful companion! Patient, unfaltering, and uncomplaining, he had given the journey his all and looked after me every step of the way. I am in awe of him, his strength, his stamina, and his calm, steady nature, but above all, I am grateful to him for giving me my dreams.

Additional Information

Total number of weeks on the road: 9 (64 days)

Total distance: 1,004 miles

Number of days spent travelling: 50

Number of days off: 14

Shortest day: 11 miles

Longest day: 28 miles

Average distance per day: 20.08 miles

Sets of shoes:
- Fronts: 3
- Hinds: 2

Number of soakings: 5

Training and Fitness:
8 weeks of gradually increasing mileage, from 3 or 4 miles a day, several times a week, to 13+ miles a day, five or six days a week.

Finding stops:
I used Google maps to look for stops. I would identify the area where we needed a stop, Google livery yards, equestrian centres or riding schools and ring those, asking if they could help us out, or if not whether they knew of anyone who could. That failing, campsites, farm B&Bs and local pubs were good places to try.

Equipment List

On me:
- Jogging bottoms
- T-shirt
- Hoodie
- Snood
- Walking boots
- Waterproofs
- Half chaps
- Bum bag containing: phones, wallet, hoof pick, tick removers, knife, multitool
- Small rucksack containing: snacks, maps
- Waterproof map case

On Taliesin:
- Australian stock saddle
- Woollen blanket
- Suba pad
- Head collar
- Lead ropes
- Nylon webbing bridle
- Hi-viz leg bands
- Hi-viz tail streamer
- Hi-viz water resistant rucksack covers for saddle bags
- Dry bags
- Bungee cords
- Trailmax pommel bags, saddle bags, and cantle bag

In the pommel bags:
- Snacks (energy bars, flap jacks, nuts etc)
- 2 x 2 litre plastic water flasks

- Life straw
- Anti bacterial wipes and gel
- Cable ties
- Bailing twine
- Spring weight measure
- Gorilla tape
- Length of thin nylon rope
- Poo bags for litter and dog etc
- Kitchen roll
- Rubber gloves
- Woollen gloves

In the cantle bag:
- Electric fencing wire
- Collapsing fence stakes (made from old fibreglass tent poles)
- Insulators
- Small fencer (Hotline Shrike)
- Brushes for Taliesin
- Light weight 2 man tent (Vango Blade 200)
- Sleeping bag (Vango Nitestar 250)
- Dog food
- Self inflating sleeping mat strapped onto the outside

In the saddle bags:
- Dog food
- 450 gram gas cartridge
- 2 small lightweight saucepans
- Food (rice, pasta, couscous, small bottle of olive oil, salt, pepper, tomato puree, several packets of spice mixes, salt and pepper)
- Fork
- Spoon
- 2 x lighters
- Notebook

- Eraser
- Pen
- Pencil
- Pencil sharpener
- Head torch
- Hand held torch
- Spare batteries for fencer and torches
- Phone chargers
- 2 x battery packs for phone
- 2 x word puzzle and Sudoku books
- Deodorant
- Nail files
- Cotton buds
- Hairbands
- Tooth brush
- Tooth paste
- Pyjama bottoms
- Long sleeve top
- Woollen vest
- 1 x set of long johns
- 1 x pair of tights
- Horse passport
- First aid kit containing: salt, calendula cream, hibi scrub, plasters, knee braces, surgical tape, sanitary towels, syringe, bute, bandages, saline wipes, dressings, Vaseline, book of equine emergency first aid.

Also by this author:

Fiddler on the Hoof

Around Ireland on Horseback with a Violin

ISBN Paperback: 9798614000134

In the summer of 2018 fiddle player and adventurer Cathleen Leonard embarked on her second major long distance journey on horseback. This time Cathleen was accompanied by her partner, Vlad – who had never ridden a horse before – along with her faithful wolfdog, Spirit, her rescued French draught horse, Oisín, and her nervous, inexperienced young horse, Dakota, who had an irrational fear of drains and people. The unlikely fellowship set off from Cornwall, travelled through the South West of England and across South Wales, then crossed the sea to Ireland where they rode from Mizen to Malin. Half way across Ireland they were joined by a small but opinionated one-eyed mule, who added even more colour to the adventure. Irish history, mythology, and music are woven into Cathleen's account of spontaneous travel and the kindness of strangers. The open hospitality of the people they meet, and the beauty of the landscapes they travel through trump the myriad and often hilarious setbacks encountered along the way.

1

Reasons

The wind was stripping dead leaves off the trees and blowing them in swirling gusts across the asphalt where a handful of familiar cars were parked. Taking a deep breath, I got out of my van and headed for the pub door. I heard the familiar click of the latch as I pushed the door open and stepped inside. It was dark in the dingy bar, a fire roared in the wood-burning stove, and brass ornaments and harness buckles glinted on the dark wooden beams. Around the tall wooden island in the middle of the bar, the usual crowd of regulars sat perched on the same stools they always occupied, drinking pints of the same beer they always drank, having the same old conversations they always had – every day of the week.

It was the twenty-eighth of October, the day after I'd returned from my nine week long, 1,000 mile solo journey from Scotland to Cornwall with my steadfast old draught horse, Taliesin. It had been the adventure of a lifetime and a childhood dream finally realised.

I'd returned quietly and reluctantly, dragging my feet and wishing I were headed anywhere but home. I hadn't wanted the adventure to end. There's something about life on the road – the simplicity and the freedom of it, coupled with the insecurity of never knowing what to expect – that makes you feel so intensely alive. But winter and bad weather had been close on our heels and Taliesin had needed a rest.

Before leaving for Scotland, I'd been working behind the bar of that little village pub. It was a typical pub in rural Cornwall in as much as it was full of staunch regulars by whose drinking habits you could set a clock. It was the sort of place where everyone knew everyone else's business and what they didn't know, they would make up. Actually, it had been long hours of pulling pints and listening to mindless gossip that had finally driven me to chase my dream of riding the length of the country. I'd been afraid that if I didn't do it I would become stuck – sucked into a rut of mundane trivia and silly village drama while life passed me by. In the end, that idea had been more terrifying than the prospect of riding alone from one end of the country to the other.

The day after my return, I'd gone to see about getting my job back; but the moment I walked through the pub door and saw the same old bunch of people, doing the same old things they always did, and having the same old conversations they always had, I knew I couldn't face it again. It made me feel as though I had never been away, as though the journey had never happened. Nothing here had changed. Not a single thing. Except me. No, I decided firmly as I turned around and headed for the door, I needed to do something more meaningful and more rewarding with my time.

A few weeks later I took up employment in the only other sector in Cornwall where there is never a shortage of work: the healthcare industry.

Long days of driving from the home of one client to the next ensued; tending to the frail and elderly, the disabled, the sick, and the dying; helping them to perform the basic daily tasks which I – in my relatively healthy twenty-seven-year-old body – naively took for granted. It was hard work, with early morning starts and late night finishes, and the pay left a lot to be desired. Although the work was far from glamorous, I enjoyed making a difference – however small – to those people's lives. I loved hearing their stories, too – the tales of their youth and life in the 'good old days'. I happily listened to the life-lessons and hard-won wisdom that they offered up in our daily encounters while I assisted them to wash and dress, prepared meals, and served endless cups of tea.

The job broadened my own perspective on life and opened my eyes to the harsh realities of sickness and old age. It taught me the valuable lesson that health and mobility should be cherished above all other things, and that neither should ever be taken for granted.

Something else happened not long after my return which further hammered home the stark lesson that nothing in life should be taken for granted, and that was my father's illness.

He had known for a while that something was wrong – he'd said as much over the phone on the few occasions I'd spoken to him on my long journey from Scotland to Cornwall. In the last week of the adventure I rang him as I was settling in for the night at a stop near Taunton. He told me he was having trouble eating and was in a lot of discomfort when he did.

'I'm worried,' he said, his voice sounding thin and weak over the phone. 'What will your mother do if something happens to me?'

Always the pessimist! I thought, rolling my eyes.

'Don't be like that, Dad. I'm sure it's nothing to worry about. You'll be fine!' I said almost flippantly.

He and mum were living in County Clare in the west of Ireland, and things over there happen slowly, so it wasn't until some time in the middle of November that he managed to get an appointment to find out what was causing the problem. More than a month passed while we waited for the results, which finally came through just days before Christmas. It wasn't something straightforward at all – it was stomach cancer.

The news was sudden and unexpected. I suppose you never really believe something like that will happen to you or your immediate loved ones. It's one of those things that happen to other people, and other families.

Yet here it was: cancer.

Another long wait for scans and an appointment with a specialist followed. It was Christmas and everything in Ireland grinds to a halt. There was nothing available until the New Year. By the time Dad finally got to see a consultant in early January 2018, it was only to be told that the cancer had spread too far to be operable. It was untreatable so they sent him home to die.

Dad wasn't going to give up that easily, though. Not without a fight first. There were alternative treatments out there – things the medical profession wouldn't acknowledge. What was the harm in trying? And so began a daily cocktail of colloidal silver, hemp oil, CBD oil, sodium bicarbonate, and a whole pile of other alternative and herbal remedies whose names and purposes I have now forgotten – all accompanied by regular healing sessions. But to no avail.

Barely able to eat, Dad gradually wasted away to nothing. He looked like a skeleton, but for fluid that was accumulating around his stomach. It needed to be drained. It was a routine procedure to make him more comfortable, they said, and they could do it at Limerick Hospice. He would be out in a day or two.

A day or two became a week, and then two. He was growing frailer by the day and was too weak to go home, the doctors said. Besides, they could care for him better in the hospice. He was starting to fade now, drifting further into his own space and time, far away from the real world; he was awake but not entirely present. I'd seen this in my work with people nearing the end of life. Our conversations over the phone gradually became more rambling and less comprehensible. It was hard to follow what Dad was saying as he wandered listlessly from one unrelated topic to the next. Every now and then he would become lucid and talk coherently for a while, before drifting off again to who-knew-where – and each time we spoke his voice sounded thinner and feebler.

Dad never left the hospice and, on the 12th of February 2018, he passed away. He was only sixty-nine years old. I was with him when he died, sitting by his bed holding his hand for the last few hours of his life, listening to each laboured breath as he struggled to escape his cumbersome, cancer-riddled body. It's a hard fight to let go at the end, and I was glad to be there, surrounded by his friends and family. It was a peaceful and painless passing, and for that I was grateful. Working with people who had spent years suffering with degenerative, and utterly debilitating illnesses had shown me all too clearly what a slow and painful death might have been – both for him, and for the rest of my family. Sometimes you have to be grateful for the small mercies.

If care work had taught me the value of health and mobility, then losing my father taught me the value of time. It reinforced my already strong determination to live life to the fullest and to dedicate whatever time I might have to the pursuit of my dreams. My personal motto: 'Do it while you can!' took on a whole new meaning.

So what was I waiting for? There was a whole world out there to explore! And the first stop, I decided, would be Ireland.

The little island on the western-most edge of Europe, with its many long-fingered peninsulas reaching into the expanse of the wild Atlantic, had always held a certain appeal for me.

Ireland was a land steeped in the myths and legends of the Celtic race, where ancient gods and heroes of times long past had played out their epic sagas. It was a place where folklore and fairy tales abounded and where people still held a strong belief in the fairy folk who wandered the hollow hills and danced around lone thorn-trees on moonlit nights; and where tinkers in horse-drawn wagons spun stories around turf fires on the roadsides.

That was a rather romantic image, so you can probably imagine how disappointed I was when, on visiting Ireland and having a good look around after my parents moved there in 2012, I found it to be … well, pretty much like any other country I'd been to. There were no wild men charging about on horseback doing battle with gods and giants, or undertaking heroic quests; no fairies frolicking about in the bushes at night, and hardly a trace of anyone wandering the mountain roads in horse-drawn wagons. Instead there were just the usual kinds of people living pretty normal lives. Yet even in the tamed and settled landscape the legends and myths lived on – immortalised in the names of the hills, the lakes, the rivers, and the sea-ravaged headlands, their ancient memory echoing down the ages.

And then there was the music! Music that held the story of the land and the people who had lived there; beautiful, evocative music! Captivating melodies that bore the names of people and places from all over Ireland, or ballads that told of the hardships and heartbreaks that had befallen men and women who were long-since dead but whose stories were kept alive through songs that had spread to the four corners of the world.

My father was Irish and I grew up listening to the music of the Dubliners, Planxty, the Chieftains, and many, many more of the artists that had helped to popularise traditional Irish music in the latter part of the 20th century. I loved the songs, and even more than that, I loved the instrumental melodies: the jigs and reels, polkas and hornpipes, airs and marches. Some say that many of the most beautiful Irish tunes were actually fairy melodies, picked up by eavesdropping mortals. I could well believe it! It was the kind of music that never failed to set your feet tapping, and brought a smile to your face. It had provided a soundtrack to my childish imaginings in which I roamed the wild hills on horseback with a wolf at my side, setting off on all kinds of epic adventures.

I wanted to discover the country that had given rise to such beautiful music and so many magical tales; I wanted to meet its people and see for myself some of the mythical places of folklore and legend; and above all – as a fiddle player – I wanted to map a musical trail across that enchanted island, discovering the tunes of the places through which we passed. What better way to do this than on horseback, immersing myself in the landscape, and putting myself at the mercy of its people?

It was time to hit the road again, and this adventure, I decided, would be a musical journey on horseback and a quest of my own to discover ancient Ireland.

Printed in Great Britain
by Amazon